BRITAIN'S
WILD FLOWERS

MEADOWSWEET
Filipendula ulmaria

BRITAIN'S WILD FLOWERS

A TREASURY OF TRADITIONS, SUPERSTITIONS, REMEDIES AND LITERATURE

ROSAMOND
RICHARDSON

 National Trust

Dedicated to the memory of
'the bard of the wild flowers'
John Clare
(1793–1864)

and in loving remembrance of my grandfather
Harold Frederick Page (1882–1983)
countryman and naturalist

First published in the United Kingdom in 2017
by National Trust Books
43 Great Ormond Street
London WC1N 3HZ

An imprint of Pavilion Books Group
Text copyright © Rosamond Richardson, 2017
Volume copyright © National Trust Books, 2017

ISBN: 9781909881921

A CIP catalogue record for this book is available from the British Library.

10 9 8 7 6 5

Reproduction by Mission, Hong Kong
Printed by 1010 Printing International Ltd, China

This book can be ordered direct from the publisher at the website:
www.pavilionbooks.com, or try your local bookshop.
Also available at National Trust shops or www.shop.nationaltrust.org.uk

The recipes and remedies in this book are historical, no longer used and
are in no way an invitation to try out past practice.

CONTENTS

INTRODUCTION

If you stay close to nature, to its simplicity, to the small things hardly noticeable, those things can unexpectedly become great and immeasurable.

RAINER-MARIA RILKE, *LETTERS TO A YOUNG POET*

'I love all wild flowers (none are weeds with me)' wrote nineteenth-century poet and naturalist John Clare. For many of us, wild flowers link to childhood, to wonder and innocence: a daisy or a dandelion may be among our earliest memories of the natural world. At a very young age, children sense the beauty and mystery of nature: wild flowers imprint on the imagination and are connected with feelings of delight and awe. The memory lingers: traditional flower-rich hay meadows, once an everyday sight and now so rare, express for many of us the soul of the countryside.

Wild flowers and human beings are old acquaintances: they have played a significant part both in our cultural history and in our wider consciousness. On a practical level, meadows have been a feature of the English landscape for centuries: they provided pastureland for livestock, grass and hay for fodder, plant matter for manure, and furze and grasses for bedding. Nectar and pollen from meadowland flowers provided essential food for pollinators of food crops. Wild plants from the fields and woods provided sustenance for the human body, too, and medicine from earliest times. Beyond that, the scope of wild flowers reaches from philosophy and history to the supernatural and trans-human worlds of mythology and magic, alchemy and religion, to the realms of science and art, botany and anthropology through to literature, legend and the fine arts.

Looking at the natural histories of wild flowers, this book explores the web of interrelationships linking us to them. In its origins, the term 'natural history' described a cross-discipline of numerous specialities encompassing scientific analysis and a broad spectrum of the humanities, including theology. A discipline of both natural and cultural components based on accurate observation and validated experience, the study of plants spanned the utilitarian to the philosophical. The plurality of 'natural history' started with Aristotle, built on an enquiry into the underlying concept of the 'Great Chain of Being', which intuited twentieth-century scientific discoveries of the atomic interconnectedness of the physical world, linking to the chain of dependency that constitutes the complex maze of ecology.

WILD FLOWERS AND MEDICINE

Fossil evidence 60,000 years old shows that Paleolithic man used plants as medicine. Sumerian clay tablets from 3000BC mention opium and myrrh as plant remedies. The first written record, from China around 2800BC, lists 366 medicinal plants, and the Ebers papyrus of 1500BC shows an in-depth knowledge of 850 plants, indicating that herbal medicine flourished in ancient Egypt.

In the Galenic and Hippocratic traditions, Nature was depicted as a 'homely woman' who removed illness from the body by affecting the elements that had caused disease, washing them from the body and bringing healthful balance and harmony: a concept of holism where treatment involved the patient not just physically, but mentally and spiritually too. Plants were believed to have powers to protect the soul from harm, and the divine magic of wild flowers required particular rituals to ensure their potency. Country superstitions sprouted, and with them a tradition of folk cures, which also encompassed the placebo effect. In perceiving the relationship between disease, health and cure, the line between the physical and the psychological was blurred – often in a useful way. The prevailing theory of 'humours', personality types based on body fluids, underlined a psychology of illness and health that, combined with everyday plant science, was to rural herb women, and men, a matter of common sense. Thus superstitions about certain plants and the manner of their gathering were grounded in a particular wisdom. The healing properties of plants even extended to livestock. In 1960 George Ewart Evans wrote in *The Horse and the Furrow* of fevers treated with agrimony, and of coughs and colds cured with feverfew, belladonna, meadow-rue and horehound. For de-worming, the horsemen used celandine, and to encourage appetite they put gentian, elecampane, horehound and felwort into the horses' feed.

Plants are nature's great chemists. Wild flowers were (and are) serious medicine. Over 50 per cent of modern prescription drugs are derived from chemical compounds first identified in plants (70 per cent of all anti-cancer drugs came originally from plant chemicals). Herbal medicines do not differ greatly from synthetic drugs in the way they work. Wild plants have proven medicinal properties: antiseptic, antispasmodic, antibacterial, antiviral, diuretic, anti-flatulent, expectorant, anti-inflammatory, antifungal. Others detoxify, bring down fevers, act as antihistamines or afford pain relief. Traditional country cures have been authenticated by scientific research: digoxin from foxgloves, aspirin from willow, colchicine from autumn crocus, opium from poppies, vincristine from periwinkle, galantamine from snowdrops, paclitaxel from yew. Even the commonest 'weeds' such as nettle, chickweed and dandelion possess compounds which have measurable biochemical effects.

After the founding of the National Health Service in Britain in the 1940s, people became dependent on synthetic drugs for everyday complaints that used to be easily and safely treated with natural remedies. Despite the burgeoning of the pharmaceutical companies that have come to dominate western medicine, this herbal knowledge survives in scattered parts of rural Europe where the production and processing of medicinal plants still flourishes, notably in Italy where ancient herbal traditions are kept alive. There are places where women still make traditional family medicines and where you can buy dried plant remedies. Centres of research in cities and towns such as Florence and San Sepulcro continue to evaluate scientifically the therapeutic value of plants in human health. Although European Union regulations for licensing and selling herbal medicines have restricted their commercial use, there are no laws against making your own. With knowledge, care and the right guidance, many plants can still be used for non-serious everyday ailments.

WILD PLANTS IN EVERYDAY LIFE

Alongside practical uses in food and drink, plant dyes, aromatics and cosmetics, whimsy found its place in rural tradition. Plants were observed to behave in particular ways in certain conditions, and became weather indicators. Others were oracles of love, or omens of disaster, or luck-bringers. The rich tradition of folklore that developed in the countryside, largely an oral one but now generally relegated to dry-as-dust tomes or the memories of grandparents and great-grandparents, is playful, imaginative and entertaining: in the mid-nineteenth century when it was still common currency, John Clare wrote in one of his 'Natural History Letters' that 'Superstition with all her deformity is a very poetical personage with me & I love to dwell on such trifles.'

THE GREAT HERBALISTS

Handing down the wisdom of specific properties of plants, whether practical, medicinal or apotropaic, was a natural part of rural life in days of a then-essential, pre-pharmaceutical knowledge of medicine. The herbals of the so-called 'Dark' Ages and medieval Europe evolved in response to this need: a lasting delight to read, they are a heady mixture of genuine science, wacky superstition and elegant prose, a tribute to the lost wisdom of an era considerably more connected to the natural world than ours. Much of the plant medicine relied on was based on writings from the early centuries of the first millennium and before: Theophrastus (*Enquiry into Plants*), Pliny the Elder (*Natural History*), Dioscorides (*De Materia Medica*), and Galen who among other writings contributed a treatise with the wonderful title *That the Best Physician is also a Philosopher.*

In the early medieval period, when Benedictine monasteries became the sole repositories of learning, monks studied these works for their centuries-old wisdom, and became default physicians to the people in their communities. They grew the raw materials in their physic gardens, drying and distilling them for myriad cures. To add to this treasure trove of knowledge, the Crusaders of the eleventh to thirteenth centuries brought back from the Middle East sophisticated plant lore from Arab traditions. Through trade routes, the medieval Islamic world had absorbed much knowledge from China, India and Persia, along with that of the Classical writers. They developed the science of pharmacology later inherited by Europe through works of, among others, Avicenna, whose *The Canon of Medicine* of 1025 remained the standard medical text book for centuries, and is one of the most famous books in the history of its subject.

From the manuscripts of the eighth to fourteenth centuries, to the printed herbals of 1470–1670, medieval and Renaissance herbals preserved the science of Islamic, Christian, Ancient Greek and Roman traditions. In the sixteenth century a notorious historical footnote, the Doctrine of Signatures, popped up, maintaining that plants resembling various parts of the body were designed by their Creator to treat ailments of that part: so the lesser celandine with its knotted tubers resembling a cluster of piles was for centuries known as pilewort, and used as a remedy. The Doctrine of Signatures also allied colour to cure: the yellow flower of the dandelion would cure jaundice; the greater celandine inflammation of the bile duct. Many of the herbals incorporate these quirky ideas in parallel with traditional and more authentic medicine. Couched in the literary conventions of their time, many of the herbals are illustrated with woodcuts, drawings, paintings and engravings, which have contributed to the great art of botanical illustration.

WILD FLOWERS IN THE LITERARY AND RELIGIOUS IMAGINATION

Given their potency, natural and supernatural and aesthetic, it's unsurprising that wild flowers are threaded through the creative and literary imagination, that their wisdom has spawned proverbs, allegories and country dictums, that floral metaphors became woven into philosophy, legend and literature, and that wild flowers with their singular mixture of physical beauty and metaphysical mystery were and are an inspiration to poets and artists. These elements make plants potent symbols: in the Bible the vine, the oak, the bramble, the laurel, the nettle and the poppy are all universal signifiers. Flowers abound in art, architecture, heraldry, rituals and sacred practices, kindling the religious imagination of mankind from the world-soul of neo-Platonism to Blake's 'the holiness of the minute particular' to Darwin's 'endless forms most beautiful' to John Clare, who went 'seeking the religion of the fields... [where] birds bees trees flowers all talked to me incessantly louder than the busy hum of men and who so wise as nature out of doors on the green grass by woods and streams under the beautiful sunny sky—daily communings with God and not a word spoken––', and to Richard Jefferies, he who breathed the wind and the wild flowers into language, who perceived 'something beyond the philosophies in the light, in the grass blades, the leaf, the grasshopper, the sparrow on the wall.'

MEADOWS OF THE MIND

To see a World in a Grain of Sand
And a Heaven in a Wild Flower,
Hold Inifinity in the palm of your hand
And Eternity in an hour.

As William Blake in *Songs of Innocence and Experience* here implies,
there is more to a wild flower than just a wild flower. Meadows of the
mind is a trope for one of the two worlds we all live in: the material
world and the world as we interpret it, the world of the imagination.
As Peter Marren pointed out in *British Wildlife* in 1995, a wildflower
meadow is:

> *a folk memory, a dreamy place of tall grass and wild*
> *flowers, willow pollards and thick hedges, haycocks,*
> *sweet scents and happy country folk drinking cider ...*
> *and preferably other angels to do all the farm work while*
> *we laze in the sun, read poetry and listen to the bees*
> *and the skylarks.*

Just the idea of a meadow is a potent force, even to those who have
never seen one. The beauty of wild flowers on a grassy bank in spring,
or covering herb-rich grassland in summer, whether for real, or in art
or film, or just as an idea, may awaken existential longing, stimulating
the human impulse to question its own mortality. With their short
lives and perennial return wild flowers are symbols of birth, life,
death, afterlife and eternity. They remind us of our ephemerality.
Through them we connect to the liminal, to the natural mysteries of
life and death and transcendence. Wild flowers confront us with the
'how' and 'why' questions of existence, to creation with its unending
cycles and innate transience. The *perpetuum mobile* of existence with its
unrepeatability, described by Richard Feynman as 'the inconceivable

nature of nature', provides a mystery that provokes in us Coleridge's 'shaping power of the imagination'. Wild flowers bridge these physical and metaphysical worlds with what Richard Jefferies called 'the alchemy of nature'. In the tiniest detail of a bird's nest, or the beauty of ivy clambering over a gatepost, he encountered the metaphysics of small things:

> *... the grass of my golden meadow has no design, and no purpose: it is beautiful, and more; it is divine.*

'The world is a mirror of absolute beauty', wrote Thomas Traherne in the seventeenth century. John Clare in the nineteenth discovered what was, for him, the 'divinity of the fields', and Jefferies wrote of 'the soul of the flowers':

> *I want the inner meaning and the understanding of the wild flowers in the meadow ... They make no shadow of pretence, these beautiful flowers, of being beautiful for my sake ... but the word soul does not in the smallest degree convey the meaning of my wish.*

CHAMOMILE
Anthemis nobilis

'Meadows matter', cries George Peterken in his definitive *Meadows* of 2013. They are safe places which represent civilisation. 'In their traditional form they are the embodiment of the pastoral ideal, the repository of memories of a pre-industrial countryside'. There is a thirst for these oases of beauty, as evidenced by naming a disproportionate number of housing estates with the tag of 'meadow'. Wild flowers meet a deep human need: as the biographer of Edward Jenner, F. D. Prewitt, wrote, 'Botanists are among these who know that, in spite of the rude shocks of life, it is well to have lived, and to have seen the everlasting beauty of the world.'

WILD FLOWERS AND WELL-BEING

Looking to the health of the natural environment, and connecting it to the spiritual well-being of the nation, the Coronation Meadows Project of 2013 celebrated the sixtieth anniversary of the Coronation of Queen Elizabeth II by identifying one 'crown jewel' meadow in every county in the UK, each destined to become a seed bank for the creation and restoration of other meadows in the same county. From the smallest site to one of 400 acres, these herb-rich pastures of native flowers will provide habitats for pollinators, and places of beauty for people, gentle, quiet places to counterbalance the noisy consumerism of the commercial world.

'To a man of dissernment [*sic*] there is happiness in contemplating the different shapes of leaves of the various kinds of trees plants and herbs   there is happiness in examining minutely into the wild flowers as we wander among them', wrote John Clare. Human beings need the beauty of nature for psychological health and a balanced perspective on life. The more our culture is divorced from nature, the more problems arise in illness, hostility, and mental disorders, including depression. Even the Victorians wrote about how the study of natural history contributed to good mental health. The historian Sir George Macaulay Trevelyan knew this for a fact, from his experience of daily walks out with nature in the Northumbrian moors and woods: 'I have two doctors: my right leg and my left.' Disconnection from nature, and ignorance of it, deprives people of elements of delight, solace and fascination that sustain the inner life. Nature Deficit Disorder now has a name – even an acronym, NDD. 'There are a great many ways of holding on to our sanity,' writes Ronald Blythe, 'amidst the vices and follies of the world, though none better than to walk knowledgeably among our native plants'.

'Long live weeds and the wilderness yet', wrote Gerard Manley Hopkins. To saunter in places where wild flowers grow can transform sadness and pain: the word saunter comes from a medieval word for pilgrims to the Holy Land or la Sainte Terre, 'sainterreurs', and these places are holy lands of sorts, replica Gardens of Eden that restore us to wholeness. Wild flowers are more than the sum of their parts, their beauty being one of the profoundest ways in which we connect and communicate with each other at moments of great joy or great grief.

> *Between My Country—and the others—*
> *There is a sea—*
> *But Flowers—negotiate between us—*
> *As Ministry*
> EMILY DICKINSON, 1864

THE INTELLIGENCE OF PLANTS

Plants are the only organisms on the planet that can lose up to 90 per cent of their bodies without being killed. This is because they have no irreplaceable organs. Rooted to the spot, plants have evolved to find everything they need, and to defend themselves, while remaining fixed in place. This they do by speaking a chemical language. A plant has three thousand chemicals in its vocabulary (while, as eminent plant biologist Stephano Mancuso remarked, 'the average student has only seven hundred words'). If, he argues, intelligence is the ability to solve problems, then plant intelligence can be defined as the ability to respond in optimal ways to challenges presented by its environment and circumstances.

Plants have evolved both short- and long-term electrical signalling, using neurotransmitter-like chemicals. They have between fifteen and twenty distinct senses, including analogues of our five: smell and taste (they sense and respond to chemicals in the air or on their bodies); sight (they react differently to various wavelengths of light as well as to shadow); touch (a vine or a root 'knows' when it encounters a solid object); and, it has been discovered, sound and volume.

They can also sense volume, nitrogen, phosphorus, salt, various toxins, microbes and chemical signals from neighbouring plants. Roots about to encounter an impenetrable obstacle or a toxic substance change course before they make contact with it. Roots can tell whether nearby roots are self or other and, if other, kin or stranger. Research on plant communication may someday benefit farmers and their crops: it's not impossible that plant-distress chemicals could be used to prime plant defences, reducing the need for pesticides.

In Darwin's work of 1880, *The Power of Movement in Plants*, he wrote that the root tip of a plant 'acts like the brain of one of the lower animals; the brain being seated within the anterior end of the body, receiving impressions from the sense organs and directing the several movements.' Darwin, who regarded nature with respect and wonder, was asking us to think of the plant as a kind of upside-down animal, with its main sensory organs and 'brain' on the bottom, underground, and its sexual organs on top!

WILD FLOWERS IN THE ECOLOGY

Meadows (and basically anywhere wild flowers grow, in hedgerows, verges, woodland, heaths or hillsides) matter at many levels, but they also matter in the wider ecology: wild flowers are a vital thread in the delicate fabric of relationships linking wild plants to the health of an environment threatened by an urbanised culture divorced from the natural world. The ecological chain is only as strong as its weakest link, and in that fact lies our inevitable interdependence on each link - including the smallest. If one breaks, the chain is broken. Small things are essential building blocks of the bigger picture, and wild flowers are fundamental to a fragile but vital relationship with invertebrates, insects and birds in the web of being: each and every one has an individual role to play, with elements that may be vital to the habitat of a goldfinch, or a silver washed fritillary butterfly, or a micro-moth, or a spider, a lizard or an earthworm. As wild plants decline, the ecological pyramid is damaged.

Eighty per cent of inhabitants of some Asian and African countries use herbal medicine for some aspects of primary healthcare: this means five billion people worldwide still rely on traditional plant medicine. It's reckoned that 400 medicinal plants are at risk of extinction from over-collection and deforestation, threatening the discovery of future cures for disease. Wild flowers are an endangered species: habitats are being obliterated by the footprint of an ever-expanding human population and the onslaught of agrochemicals. Ninety-seven per cent of Britain's meadows were lost between the 1930s and 1980s, encroached upon by what John Clare called 'the human ant hill'. Our lanes used to be thick with wild flowers, now the cornflower and the corn cockle have as good as disappeared, but you only have to go to rural Eastern Europe to see what a less populated landscape looks like without agrochemicals – which also, of course, are absorbed into the raw material of our food and drink via the soil and water-table. Mourning such lost landscapes, Roger Deakin, in *Notes from Walnut Tree Farm*, described how:

> *I walk about the common with my imaginary medieval friend.*
> *'The ponds are so shallow. Why are they nearly dried out?' he*
> *says, amazed at the state of the grass. 'What's happened to all*
> *the cowslips and buttercups – and the hay rattle flowers? Where*
> *are the clouds of butterflies that used to rise up before the scythe?*

Many of our wild flowers are ancestors of garden plants – poppy, hellebore, bistort, foxglove and many others – and some wild plants can contribute beauty to a herbaceous border or cottage garden without risk of invasion: cowslips, forget-me-not, borage or bluebells for example can all play their part in a managed plot of land. They are all beautiful: of our 1,407 native species, 20 per cent of them are threatened: let us cherish them, and never take them for granted. Richard Jefferies posits an imaginary scenario:

> *If we had never before looked upon the earth, but suddenly*
> *came to it man or woman grown, set down in the midst of*
> *a summer mead, would it not seem to us a radiant vision?*
> *The hues, the shapes, the song and life of birds, above all the*
> *sunlight, the breath of heaven, resting on it; the mind would*
> *be filled with its glory, unable to grasp it, hardly believing*
> *that such things could be mere matter and no more. Like a*
> *dream of some spirit land it would appear, scarce fit to be*
> *touched lest it should fall to pieces, too beautiful to be watched*
> *lest it should fade away.*

Before it does, we must protect disappearing habitats, even if this endeavour seems like 'tilting at impossible windmills', in Miriam Rothschild's words.

'If I live I will write ... a garden of wild Flowers as it shall contain nothing else with quotations from poets and others   an English Botany on this plan would be very interesting..'. So wrote John Clare in his *Journal* on Sunday 24 October 1824. But he never did write his garden of wild flowers, to our great loss. He had another scheme that never came to fruition either: in a letter to his publisher John Taylor, he proposed writing the 'biographies of wild flowers'. One hundred and fifty years after his death, this twenty-first-century version tells the stories and histories of the best-known and best-loved of our British flora, and is dedicated to his memory: the genius poet-naturalist John Clare (1793–1864), self-styled 'bard of the wild flowers, Rain-washed and wind-shaken', whose lines from 'Child Harold' conjure a lost landscape:

> *The paigles bloom in showers in grassy close*
> *How sweet to be among their blossoms led*
> *& hear sweet nature to herself discourse*
> *While pale the moon is bering over head*
> *& hear the grazeing cattle softly tred*
> *Cropping the hedgerows newly leafing thorn——*
> *Sounds soft as visions murmured oer in bed*
> *As dusky eve or sober silent morn*
> *For such delights twere happy man was born.*

CORNFLOWER
Centaurea cyanus

FIELD POPPY
Papaver rhoeas

The wild flowers: From Agrimony to Yarrow

*Botanick Studies have a native Tendency to the
Support, Comfort, and Delight of Mankind.*

Caleb Threlkeld, Irish field botanist, 1727

22

AGRIMONY

Agrimonia eupatoria, A. procera

Delicate spikes of yellow stars appear along the verges after midsummer, slender agrimony. Flowering along the lanes of East Anglia during and after harvest, and on grassy roadsides, woodland edges, meadows and hedgerows, agrimony is commoner in the south than in the north of Britain. Medieval monks grew 'the great healer' in infirmary gardens: Walafrid Strabo wrote, in his *Hortulus* or 'Little Garden' of the ninth century, 'here in handsome rows you can see my agrimony. It clothes all the fields with its profusion; it grows wild in the woodland shade. If crushed and drunk, the draught will check the most violent stomach ache.'

Colloquially 'nun of the fields', the French called it Philanthropos and dedicated it to St Guillaume. The leaves could be made into a compress for open wounds – 'being beaten small when it is green, it hath power to cure cuts' – and even wounded deer were supposed to be healed by grazing on agrimony. A further use was found for it: place agrimony under your pillow and you will have a sound night's sleep, as in an eleventh-century poem:

> *If it be leyd under mann's heed*
> *He shal sleepyn as he were deed,*
> *He shal nevere drede ne wakyn*
> *Till from under his head it be takyn.*

Agrimony's generic name eupatoria refers to Mithradates Eupator, king of ancient Persia in the first century BC whose fame as an herbalist rested on his experiments on himself. He took sub-lethal doses of poisonous plants, searching for their antidotes, believing he could find a universal one for all toxins. He so effectively immunised himself that when he was captured by Pompey and was in danger of being killed, his attempt to poison himself failed (he finally turned to his friend and bodyguard and asked him to kill him with his sword). The 'universal antidote' he is said to have invented became known as the 'mithridate', a semi-mythical cocktail with between fifty and sixty ingredients. It became highly sought after in the Middle Ages and used as a remedy for the plague, among other things. An almond-sized amount taken in wine would, it was claimed, counteract all poisons.

One of the 57 herbs in the Anglo-Saxon 'Holy Salve', agrimony became a potent 'simple', an herb used singly as opposed to being compounded with others. Chaucer recommended 'egrimoyne' for 'a bad back and alle wounds'. It was an ingredient of *eau de arquebusade*, used for staunching wounds, after a fifteenth-century word for musket or arquebus, and recent experiments in China have established its blood-staunching and anti-inflammatory effects. Principally, though, agrimony was used to cure cataracts: its generic name *Agrimonia* comes from the Greek *argemon* meaning a white speck on the cornea, therefore a plant beneficial for the eyes.

Country herbalists claimed it would also cure a range of ills from poisonous snake bites to sore throats, gout to colic, earache to cancers, warts to poor sight and memory loss, cold sores to bites and stings, earaches and colds to chilblains and piles, fevers and pre-menstrual tension to nosebleeds. Regarded as a cure-all, agrimony was specifically, according to John Gerard's *Herbal* of 1597, a fount of all wisdom in matters pertaining to wild flowers, 'good for those that have naughtie livers', a claim most likely by association with the yellow colour of the flowers. Culpeper maintained that it would draw out 'thorns and splinters of wood, nails, or any other such thing gotten into the flesh', and was also 'a most admirable remedy for those

> *Place agrimony under your pillow and you will have a sound night's sleep*

whose lives are annoyed either by heat or by cold'.

A fragrant, faintly apricot-scented tea made from agrimony is known in folk medicine for relieving colds. It can be drunk as a spring tonic and cleanser, or used externally for skin conditions. The plant contains tannins and has astringent and styptic properties: and it is still prescribed today by European herbalists for mild diarrhoea, as a gargle for oral and throat infections, and as a remedy for bedwetting. Agrimony wine was prescribed for colds. The whole plant yields a yellow dye.

With its relative *A. procera*, which is slightly taller and larger, *A. eupatoria* is a perennial member of the rose family. In the language of flowers agrimony stands for faithfulness. It's also known as church steeples, fairy rod, fairy-wand, tea-plant, rats' tails, cockle-bur (from the seeds which hook on to clothing), lemonade flower and liverwort. A perennial pollinated by a variety of small insects (or self-pollinated), agrimony is the food plant of the grizzled skipper and the large grizzled skipper butterflies and the *Stigmella splendissimella* and *aurella* moths. Its relative hemp agrimony (*Eupatorium cannabinum*) is the food plant of five *Lepidoptera* including the hemp-agrimony plume and the lime-speck pug moths.

ALEXANDERS
Smyrnium olusatrum

S hining green and gold along spring hedgerows, especially along the Eastern coastline, beautiful *Smyrnium olusatrum* with its glossy leaves is one of the first umbellifers to appear in spring. The Romans called it parsley of Alexandria (Galen underlining its culinary rather than medicinal value), and it was they who introduced it into Britain. It was eventually planted in medieval infirmary gardens when it was known as rock parsley of Alexandria, *Petroselinum alexandrium*. A native of the Mediterranean and primarily a shoreline plant, alexanders is still found growing among the ruins of monastic houses.

It was from earliest times an official medicinal herb: fresh juice from the root and seed was used on cuts and wounds in much of Europe until as recently as the 1830s. 'The leaves bruised and applied to any bleeding wound, stoppeth the blood and dryeth up the sore without any griefe', wrote seventeenth-century botanist and herbalist William Coles in his *The Art of Simpling*. Alexanders seed soaked in wine was formerly considered an emmenagogue, to stimulate menstrual bleeding, and the leaves used as an antiscorbutic against scurvy in the days when vitamin C extracts were unavailable. The roots are mildly diuretic, and the bitter taste of the leaves sharpens the appetite.

Alexanders was equally important as a culinary pot-herb from the first until the eighteenth centuries, grown like celery, blanched to remove the bitterness of the mature green parts of the plant. The leaves, upper parts of the roots, and the flower-buds were all eaten until the plant was superseded by celery. It has bright green, three-lobed leaves and yellow-green flower-heads in early spring, which can be steamed and eaten like sprouting broccoli. John Evelyn recommended alexanders for the 'Kitchin-Garden', and in his *Acetaria* of 1699 includes the yellow-green flower-buds as an ingredient for salads: they can be eaten raw and have a pleasant, nutty taste. 'The gentle fresh sprouts, buds, and tops are to be chosen, and the stalks eaten in the spring; and when blanch'd, in winter likewise, with oyl, pepper, salt, etc by themselves, or in composition: They make also an excellent vernal pottage.' He was not the only one to think so: 'Our Allisanders are much used', wrote John Parkinson in his 1640 *Theatricum Botanicum*, 'in the time of Lent, to helpe to digest the crudities and viscous humours gathered in the stomach, by the much use of fish at that time'. Up until the eighteenth century in Ireland, the plant was an ingredient of 'Lenten pottage', a gruel eaten during Lent and made with alexanders, watercress and nettles.

Alexanders has local names of black lovage, wild celery and horse parsley. The plant is native to beautiful wild Macedonia, Alexander the Great's birthplace: there's even a legend that he discovered it. Alexanders gets its generic name *Smyrnium* from the Greek for 'myrrh', because of its fragrant aroma. *Olus* means 'vegetable', and *atrum* 'black', from the colour of its ripe fruits.

ANGELICA

Angelica archangelica

Aflower of the metaphysical, this plant of angelic qualities is endowed with a country name of holy ghost. A subspecies of the wild angelica, *A. sylvestris*, its medicinal properties were allegedly revealed to a monk by the Archangel Michael during an outbreak of plague, hence *archangelica*. It comes into flower around 8 May, the feast day commemorating the apparition of St Michael to a bishop in Apulia in which the Archangel requested that a church be built in honour of the Holy Angels. The divine mysteries have been celebrated there ever since, and Monte Sant'Angelo at Gargano, the oldest shrine in Western Europe dedicated to St Michael, is now a World Heritage site.

Angelica archangelica grows in damp soil, often near rivers or in low-lying meadows and woods. It grows up to two metres tall, with a hollow stem seized on by children to turn into toy flutes. However, angelica is similar in appearance to several poisonous species such as hogweed, so correct identification is important. The flowers, which blossom from July onwards, are yellowish-white or greenish in colour, and grouped into large globular umbels bearing buff-yellow, flattened seeds. It has finely toothed, serrated leaves, and the starburst flowers are pollinated by a wide variety of insects. The increasingly rare swallowtail butterfly lays its eggs on angelica, as well as its relatives fennel and wild carrot, and the unrelated milkweed (*Asclepias tuberosa*). Eleven moths are known to feed on angelica, including the white-spotted pug.

Elegant, stately angelica is unique amongst the *Umbelliferae* for its scent, a perfume entirely different from that of its cousins fennel, parsley, anise, caraway and chervil. One ancient writer compares it to musk, another to juniper. It has an incense-like quality and Laplanders crowned their poets with it in the belief that its aroma would inspire verse. Even the roots are fragrant, and they form one of the principal ingredients of the European perfumery industry.

Laplanders crowned their poets with it in the belief that its aroma would inspire verse

From the tenth century on, angelica was cultivated both as a vegetable and as medicinal plant, achieving popularity particularly in Scandinavia where it grows wild. It has been used there as a flavouring agent from the twelfth century, and the Norwegians still use angelica root in bread-baking. Naturalised in Greenland, the Faroe Islands and Iceland, it's now widely cultivated in France where the long, bright green, fleshy stems are used in confectionery, candied for cake and dessert decoration, and to add flavour to jam. All parts of the plant are edible: angelica leaves can be steamed with fish, or added to spinach, or used sparingly in salads. Blanched, you can eat the stems like celery. Angelica is one of the ingredients used to flavour Chartreuse and Benedictine, as well as Vermouth and Dubonnet. The plant produces a yellow dye.

Angelica has other uses too: in his 1905 *Meals Medicinal*, the physician Dr W. T. Fernie wrote, 'The candied stems as sold by our confectioners, are of excellent service to relieve the flatulence of weakly digestion. They smell pleasantly of musk, being a capital tonic, and carminative. Furthermore they are antiseptic.' Chewing the stems does indeed, according to some, reduce flatulence, but Dr Fernie makes further claims: according to him, angelica was a traditional remedy for infectious diseases. He quotes the *Speculum Mundi* of 1643: 'Contagious aire ingendering pestilence infects not those, who in their mouths have taine Angelica, that happy counterbane'.

It has helped smokers to give up tobacco, by chewing on the seeds

This claim was taken up by John Parkinson, last of the great Renaissance herbalists, apothecary to King James I and Royal Botanist to Charles I: 'the whole plant, both leafe, roote and seede, is of an excellent comfortable scent, savour and taste ... [it is] so goode an herbe that there is no part thereof but is of much use'. It was used as a remedy for cholera and poisoning, and in the Great Plague of 1660 people chewed angelica seeds to avoid infection, believing it could cure them. 'It cureth the bitings of madde dogges and al other venomous beasts', declares Gerard, characteristically undermining credibility with overstatement. A cleansing herb, too, and good for the skin, angelica may possibly deter those inclined to overindulgence: 'Angelica taken somewhat freely as a sweetmeat will create 'a disgust for spiritous liquors', as Dr W. T. Fernie put it in the early twentieth century in his *Herbal Simples*. If drink isn't the problem, but you have toothache or bad breath, then Richard Surflet offers this advice in *The Countrie Farme* of 1600: 'The root put into a hollow tooth asswageth the paine: being chawed, it maketh the breath sweet, and concealeth the smell of garlicke, or any other suche meate which causes an ill breath.' For those with another problem altogether, here's Parkinson again: 'the dryed roots made into pouder, and taken in wine or other drinke, will abate the rage of lust in young persons.'

In folk medicine, angelica has been used to ease bronchitis, to stimulate liver function, and as a remedy for brain and head complaints. It was applied to painful joints, and used for nervousness, vertigo and fatigue. Herbalists knew it as a warming tonic to improve poor circulation, and Laplanders prescribed it for colic, for which it was one of their chief remedies. An extract of the root is anti-inflammatory, and the roots, stems and seeds were used for respiratory complaints. Simply burning the root and inhaling the fumes was found to relax mind and body, simultaneously activating the imagination and relieving depression. It has helped smokers to give up tobacco, by chewing on the seeds instead of applying nicotine patches. 'The consumption of angelica tea temporarily changes the taste [for nicotine]. It calms the nerves and helps in moments of craving.' More fancifully, if you wore angelica around your neck it would act as a charm to protect you from witches and their spells.

Angelica is commonly known as angel plant, wild parsnip, masterwort, Jack jump-about, lingwort, wild celery, bellyache root and Norwegian angelica. It is the plant above all others to have in your garden, according to the contemporary Australian herbalist Harald Tietze: 'Angelica aligns you to walk with your guardian angel. If you have space for only one plant in the garden plant the Angelica.' So I did, and it thrives. So, I hope, does my guardian angel.

32

BETONY

Stachys officinalis

Thy wild woad on each road we see
And medicinal betony...
JOHN CLARE, *COWPER GREEN*, 1828

'Sell your coat and buy betony' advises plant lore, because this wild flower is as good for the body as it is for the soul, an Italian proverb extolling its qualities: 'May you have more virtues than betony'. It has had extravagant claims made for it since Ancient Greece and the first-century Roman physician Pliny. Antonius Musa, physician to the emperor Augustus, asserted that betony would cure no less than 47 disorders. Called holy salve and believed to ward off diseases, it continued to be much used by Anglo-Saxon apothecaries. In the sixteenth century William Turner wrote, 'It would seem a miracle to tell what experience I have had of it ... [It] is appropriated to the head and eyes, for the infirmities whereof it is excellent, as also for the breast and lungs; being boiled in milk, and drunk, it takes away pains in the head and eyes ... Some write it will cure those that are possessed with devils, or frantic, being stamped and applied to the forehead.' More prosaically, Gerard considered 'it maketh a man to pisse well', and in his Herbal of 1597 gives it as 'a remedy against the bitings of madde dogges and venemous serpents, being drunk, and also applied to the hurts, and is most singular against poisons.' Culpeper is more measured: 'A very precious herb, that's certain, and most fitting to be kept in a man's house both in Syrup, Conserve, Oyl, ointment and Plaister.'

Betony's effectiveness against a hangover seems a general favourite in folk medicine, so long as the plant was cut in August but not with an iron tool. *The Grete Herball* of 1526 even recommends to 'take and eat betony ... and you shall not be drunk that day', also giving a remedy of betony in wine 'for them that ben to ferfull'. Betony was prescribed as an antidote to madness, and the Anglo-Saxon *Leech Book* of Bald declares 'it shields him against monstrous nocturnal visitors and against frightful visions and dreams'. Some people wore amulets of betony for protection, or placed one under the pillow at night.

In herbal medicine, betony was an ingredient of 'Pistoja powder', given as a remedy for backache and lumbago, arthritis and gout. Betony tea or tincture was prescribed as a nerve tonic to calm, to relax and to relieve stress, and given for insomnia. Fresh betony leaves laid on the forehead and covered with a damp cloth would ease a nervous headache, even a migraine. The herb is good for concentration and memory, and was given as a tonic for underweight children. A fifteenth-century manuscript says 'the juyce of betayne medled with oyl of rosys' would heal you of 'many divers siknesse'. Dried betony is an ingredient in herbal tobacco and snuff, together with coltsfoot and eyebright.

Potent in medicine, betony acquired a reputation as a magical and holy plant, and one of its names is bishop's wort. Betony was frequently grown in monastery gardens as well as in churchyards where it can still be found, grown to protect the living from ghosts of the dead. Wounded animals (particularly stags) that ate betony were healed, and medieval folklore tells how it was believed to affect snakes. Betony had power over witchcraft and wicked spirits too, so if you plant betony in the garden the occupants of your house will come to no harm.

A downy perennial with an upright habit, betony grows 30 to 60cm tall in high summer, with light purple flowers in dense whorls on a spike, in woods and hedgerows all over England (but not in Scotland). It came to England with the Normans in the eleventh century. Also widely known also as wood betony, in French it is *bétoine*, and in Old English was known as betayne or beteyne. The generic *Stachys* comes from the Greek for 'a spike', after the flowerhead, and *officinalis* means that it was listed as an official medicinal herb. 'Betony' may come from the Vettones, pre-Roman Celtic peoples of the Iberian peninsula who are said to have discovered betony's properties. Or, it derives from two Celtic words: *bew* meaning 'head', and *ton* meaning 'improve'.

Betony then is a woundwort, closely related to Hedge Woundwort (*Stachys sylvatica*), a wound-healer with a local name of all-heal: Culpeper regarded hedge woundwort as 'second to none' as a vulnerary or wound herb, since it heals tissues, staunches bleeding, is antiseptic, antispasmodic and sedative. It is even uplifting to the spirits: 'a distilled water of the flowers makes the heart merry, to make a good colour in the face, and to make the vitall spirits more fresh and lively.' A standard remedy of the country medicine-chest for cuts and minor wounds, hedge woundwort was made into a poultice of ointment and is now known to contain a vaporisable antiseptic oil. Gerard called it clown's all heal, and tells this tale: 'It chanced that a poore man in mowing of Peason did cut his leg with a sithe, wherein he made a wound to the bones, and withall very large and wide, and also with great effusion of bloud; the poor man crept unto this herbe, which he bruised with his handes, and tied a great quantity of it unto the wound with a piece of his shirt, which presently staunched the bleeding, and ceased the paine, insomuch that the poore man presently went to his days work againe, and so did from day to day, without resting one day until he was perfectly whole, which was accomplished in a few dayes... I saw the wound, and offered to heale the same fro charitie; which he refused, saying that I could not heale it so well as himselfe: a clownish answer I confesse, without any thanks to me for my goodwill; whereupon I have named it Clownes Woundwort.'

Hedge woundwort is the food plant of seven moths including the brindled plume, the small rivulet and the beautiful golden.

BIRD'S FOOT TREFOIL

Lotus corniculatus

'Yellow with birdfoot trefoil are the grass glades' wrote George Meredith of this abundant grassland wild flower, which, with its three-lobed leaves, is a symbol of the Trinity. Known as crow-toes, too, and God Almighty's thumb and finger, bird's foot trefoil has attracted over 70 seemingly unrelated folk names including lady's shoes and stockings, butter and eggs, bacon and eggs (after the red flushes on the yellow flowers), hop o' my thumb and goblin's fingers. Its seed pods shaped like little horns (hence *corniculatus*) account for animal's claws, toes and feet, feet of the evil cat or fingers of the devil. These pods resemble a bird's claw, too, hence bird's claw, and its commonest name of all, bird's foot.

'Trefoil' describes the crowning leaf, the others being set in pairs up the stem. The dramatic red and black six-spot burnet moth nectars on the flowers, and the plant is pollinated by bees or wasps. In all, bird's foot trefoil supports 132 different species of insect – one of nature's 'endless facts most beautiful', to paraphrase Darwin. As well as the six-spot burnet, it is an important wild flower for twenty-one other moths including the latticed heath and the chalk carpet. It is the primary food plant of the green hairstreak, dingy skipper, clouded yellow, short-tailed blue, silver-studded blue and wood white butterflies, and the secondary of the common blue. bird's foot trefoil has been grown in the past as a forage plant for pasture, hay and silage.

> *To the Romans, to wear a crown made with trefoil leaves was a high honour*

To the Romans, to wear a crown made with trefoil leaves was a high honour, presumably associated with war, since it's one of only a very few flowers to have negative connotations in the language of flowers, standing for revenge or retribution. Yet its Latin name means 'lily of the lotus-eaters', and Victorian nature writer Richard Jefferies waxes lyrical about this little flower. In *The Open Air* he wrote, 'In the mind all things are written in pictures – there is no alphabetical combination of letters and words; all things are pictures and symbols. The bird's-foot lotus is the picture to me of sunshine and summer, and of that summer in the heart which is known only in youth, and then not alone. No words could write that feeling: the bird's foot trefoil writes it.'

BISTORT

Persicaria bistorta (syn. Polygonum bistorta)

Common bistort thrives in damp meadows, wetlands and alder carr, especially in the North West of Britain. Flushing the grass with soft pink spikes from May to July, an amphibious version, *P. amphibium*, has long-stalked leaves that float on the surface of the water, and is found in shallow ponds and ditches. With a curling snake-like root, and nicknames of adder weed, adderwort and snake weed, bistort acquired by association the ability to cure snake bites. Carrying a sprig of bistort was believed to attract wealth, and if you burned the leaves with frankincense it would heighten the psychic powers of clairvoyants. An infusion of bistort was sometimes sprinkled in the house to drive out poltergeists and evil spirits.

Bistort has the reputation of being a wound herb. The root has a high tannin content and is one of the most astringent of all herbs, so a poultice quickly staunches the flow of blood and contracts body tissue. In folk medicine an infusion was used as a gargle for oral infections and sore throats, repairing the gums and relieving mouth ulcers. Bistort tea was prescribed for diarrhoea, and was used as a douche for excessive vaginal discharge. It made an ointment for piles, and was prescribed internally for peptic ulcers, ulcerative colitis, gastrointestinal disorders and occasionally in cystitis. Culpeper recommended it as a cure for toothache.

The high tannin content means the root was used in tanning leather. It contains starch, too, and can be roasted and eaten as a vegetable (once a common practice in Russia), or made into bread flour. The young leaves can be eaten in salads, or cooked like spinach. *The Grete Herball* of 1526 says that bistort 'hath vertue ... to cause to retayne and conceyve', for women who wished to have children, and gives this recipe: 'To helpe to conceyve, make an electuary of powdre of bistorte in quantyte of halfe a pounde, and swete smellynge spyces of the same weight'. And so bistort acquired the name of best birth pudding. Some even believed you had only to carry a sprig of bistort to help conception. The plant is a symbol of the consummation of marriage, and is one of the flowers of fertility depicted on the Unicorn Tapestries woven for the marriage of François the First of France and his wife Claude, Duchess of Brittany, in 1514.

Bistort is one of the dominant ingredients of a dish called Easter Ledger pudding, traditionally made in the Lake District and eaten at Passiontide – specifically the last two days of Lent, hence another local name of passiondock. Full of iron and vitamins, it was a plant to cleanse the blood after long winters when fresh greens were scarce. It's a steamed pudding made with nettles and dandelion, which are also cleansing herbs, with lady's mantle and oatmeal and barley. This dish lends its name to other nicknames for bistort: Easter ledges, Easter mangiant and Easter mentgions.

'Bistort' comes from the Latin for 'twice-twisted', after the contorted rhizome.

BLUEBELL

Hyacinthoides non-scripta (syn. Endymion non-scriptus)

*I do not think I have ever seen anything more beautiful than the bluebell ...
I know the beauty of our Lord by it. Its inscape is strength and grace.*
GERARD MANLEY HOPKINS, JOURNAL, 1870

Gazing at carpets of bluebells in early spring is to have your
eyes bathed by a violet-blue unknown in any other flower.
As Gerard Manley Hopkins puts it in his *Journal*, they grow
'in falls of sky-colour washing the brows and slacks of the ground
with vein-blue ... [where] wood banks and brakes wash wet like
lakes'. He also noted their 'faint honey smell'. The bells of bluebells
ring at daybreak to call fairies back to the woods, and if you walk
among bluebells the fairies will enchant you away. Apparently, if you

wear bluebells you will be incapable of lying, and if you dream of them you will enjoy a passionate but strong relationship.

The bells of bluebells ring at daybreak to call fairies back to the woods

Originally classified as a hyacinth, Linnaeus specified the bluebell as *non-scriptus*, because it lacks the markings on hyacinth petals said to represent the Greek '*ai, ai*' meaning 'woe, woe'. According to this legend the beautiful prince Hyacinthus had two lovers, Apollo and Zephyrus, god of the west wind. Jealous of Apollo for being the favourite, Zephyrus sought revenge. When Apollo and Hyacinthus were playing quoits, Zephyrus blew one off course and it killed Hyacinthus. Stricken with grief, Apollo raised from the spilled blood a flower that would bear his lover's name, with the marks of his anguish on its petals.

William Turner in *The Names of Herbes* of 1548 was the first to record the bluebell as we know it, and half a century later the herbalist John Gerard named it *Hyacinthus anglicus*, 'for that it is thought to grow more plentifully in England than elsewhere'. Which it does, all over Britain during April and May in deciduous woodland. The bluebell, beauty of the springtime woods with its elongated bell flowers on a drooping leafless stem, can vary in colour from azure to lilac, even to a pure white form that flourishes in my cottage garden among the springtime bulbs. These variations must be distinguished from the Spanish bluebell, *H. hispanica*, which has larger, paler blue flowers that grow all the way around an upright stem, not on just one side of a drooping stalk as with the native species. However, these two species often hybridise, so the definition is not always clear.

National favourite and logo of the Botanical Society of the British Isles, the English bluebell has a chequered botanical past, providing a bewildering study into the ways plants get their names. Linnaeus's *Hyacinthus non-scriptus* was overruled by eighteenth-century botanists who decided to categorise hyacinths separately from scillas (scilla comes from the Greek *skhizo*, to split, after the bulb that splits easily into scales). The bluebell became *Scilla nutans*, because of its nodding flower-heads, then variously *H. agraphis* ('not marked'), *Scilla non-scripta*, and *Endymion non-scriptus*. The myth of Endymion – or one of several – was that he was a son of Zeus, and of surpassing beauty. The moon goddess Selene fell in love with him, and persuaded Zeus to allow him to choose whatever he wanted. He chose to sleep for ever, deathless and ageless, on Mount Latmus (among the bluebells, perhaps?). In the 1930s, the plant was transferred back to the *Hyacinthoides* genus, and the bluebell is now officially *H. non-scripta*.

In Scotland, just to confuse the issue, harebells (*Campanula rotundifolia*) are known as bluebells. To befuddle it further, Gerard called *Endymion non-scriptus* 'harebell' too. The name 'bluebell' doesn't seem to have been much used before 1800, and even then it wasn't quick to catch on: John Clare writes in one of his 'Natural History Letters' of spring 1825, long before harebells come into flower, 'I took a walk today to botanize ... & the hare bells are just venturing to unfold their blue drooping bells ...'. He also tells a charming bluebell tale, a gardener's story from his thatched cottage in Helpston: he had placed 'the old Frog ... that has been there this four years I know it by a mark which it recieved from my spade 4 years ago I thought it woud dye of the wound so I turnd it up on a bed of flowers at the end of the garden which is thickly covered with ferns and bluebells & am glad to see it has recoverd––'.

Bluebell bulbs contain a starch second only to that of *Arum maculatum* or lords and ladies, used to stiffen ruffs in Elizabethan England before the development of cornflour. William Turner recorded that boys in sixteenth-century Northumberland, where he lived, 'scrape the roote of the herbe and glew theyr arrowes and bokes with that slyme that they scrape off'. The gummy secretion was indeed employed as bookbinders' gum, and Gerard mentions its use for setting feathers on arrows too. Bluebell juice, says Tennyson, was used to cure snake bites – and is chemically very potent, containing 15 biologically active compounds that protect the plant against animals and insects. It is in fact poisonous when fresh, the glycosides similar to those found in foxglove's digitalin. In large doses (as with foxgloves), bluebells can be toxic. The bulb has however found uses in country medicine for its diuretic and styptic properties: 'There is hardly a more powerful remedy for leucorrhoea', wrote Sir John Hill (1716–75).

The chequered skipper butterfly nectars on bluebells, which also provide food for several moths

Bluebell bulbs contain a starch second only to that of Arum maculatum or Lords and Ladies, used to stiffen ruffs in Elizabethan England before the development of cornflour

including the six-striped rustic and the autumnal rustic. The bluebell was originally known locally as crowfoot, crow flower, crow's legs and other variations on crows, as recorded by William Turner in *The Names of Herbes* in 1548. It has also acquired nicknames such as blue bonnets and blue trumpets, cuckoo flower, bell bottle, blue bottle, blue goggles, adder bell, ring o'bells, crake-feet, wood bells and wild hyacinth. Blue of the wood comes from Wales and, quaintly from Somerset, griggles.

BORAGE

Borago officinalis

When talking of borage this much is clear
That it warms the heart and brings good cheer.

Borage is *the* happiness-plant, according to praises showered on it over centuries — mostly for its alleged properties of being able to lift man's spirits and cheer him up. Following an ancient proverb *Ego borago gaudia semper ago* (I, borage, bring always courage), herbalists recommended that the flowers be put into wine to make people merry, claiming that they eliminate sadness and 'melancholy'. Pliny called borage *euphrosinum*, 'because it maketh a man merry and joyful' and Albertus Magnus referred to the plant as 'a maker of good blood'. Maybe there's something in it: borage remains today the traditional decoration for wine cups and especially Pimms, its brilliant blue, starry flowers associated with light-hearted summer celebrations. John Evelyn wrote that 'sprigs of borage in wine ... are of known Vertue to revive the Hypochondriac and chear the hard Student'. Cobalt-blue (sometimes white) flowers dazzle among the soft grey-green leaves of this lovely annual, which self-seeds freely in cottage gardens in late summer, attracting bees. They can be used to decorate salads, too, or soups, and as Parkinson points out, 'the gallant blew floures' have 'alwaies been enterposed among the flowers of women's needlework'.

The country housewife used to candy the bright flowers in syrup and rosewater before serving them dipped in icing sugar. There's an Elizabethan recipe for a tart made with apples and borage flowers, and the cucumber-tasting leaves make delicious fritters. Fresh, they can be added to cheese sandwiches, or put into homemade lemonade. For a summer wine cup, a couple of lemons can be simmered with a little sugar and borage leaves before adding to a bottle of wine (the fresh juice of the leaves and stems contain as much as 30 per cent potassium, as well as amino acids and minerals such as nitrate of potash, substances apparently libidinous as well as cheering).

Syrup made of the floures of Borage comforteth the heart, purgeth melancholy and quieteth the phrenticke and lunaticke person

Borage became an official medicinal herb, used for weak hearts, to cool fevers, to calm delirium, and applied as a poultice to relieve inflammations. The plant has a high mucilage content and in herbal medicine has been prescribed as a demulcent for soothing respiratory irritations. It is a good emollient for inflamed skin, eczema and chronic skin conditions. Oil from the seeds is prescribed for pre-menstrual tension, and the leaves are diuretic.

In the late sixteenth century, Francis Bacon says of borage 'if in the must of wine, while it worketh, before it be tunned, the Borage stay a short time, and be changed with fresh, it will make a sovereign drink for melancholy passion' (shorthand for depression). Gerard enlarges: 'Those of our time do use the flowers in salads, to exhilirate and make the mind glad. There be also many things made of them, used every where for the comfort of the heart, for the driving away of sorrow, and increasing the joy of the minde. Syrup made of the floures of Borage comforteth the heart, purgeth melancholy and quieteth the phrenticke and lunaticke person'. Yet another affirmation of its anti-depressant properties, extolled in verse by Richard Burton in *The Anatomy of Melancholy*:

> *Borage and hellebore fill two scenes,*
> *Sovereign plants to purge the veins*
> *Of melancholy, and cheer the heart*
> *Of those black fumes which make it smart.*

'Borage for courage', goes an old saying (*cor-ago*, 'I stimulate the heart'). Borage probably gets its name from the medieval Latin *burra*, meaning 'rough hair' or a 'shaggy garment', after its hairy leaves, and one of the plant's commonest local names is burrage. A thirteenth-century French name is *bourrache*, and the plant has a local English nickname of beebread.

BUGLE

Ajuga reptans

When purple bugles peeped in woods
'Neath darkest shades that boughs and leaves could make

JOHN CLARE

'It is a blacke herbe and it groweth in shaddowy places and moyst groundes' writes William Turner of this creeping plant, which, according to Gerard, was as widely planted in gardens in his day as it is in ours, since it makes for excellent ground cover in damp shady corners. Bugles are an important nectar source for the chequered skipper butterfly, and for all the fritillaries, and are visited by and cross-fertilised by bees. With nicknames of babies' shoes, horse and hounds, carpetweed and bugle weed, the purplish-blue flower spikes have also been called thunder and lightning, describing the dramatic juxtaposition of dark and light colours on each corolla (the sheen of the dark leaves is likened poetically by some to light through rain). In Germany, if you pick bugle and bring the flowers indoors it was believed it would cause a fire.

Bugle is above all else a healing plant, a vulnerary, sharing with self heal a local name of carpenters' herb, and likewise used as a remedy for occupational injuries. Like comfrey it was used to mend broken bones, was applied to wounds and bruises, and was prescribed internally for ulcers. Herb women made an infusion for haemorrhages, coughs, and the spitting of blood, and used it to lower blood pressure and as 'one of the best narcotics in the world' (apparently it also counteracted the effects of overconsumption of alcohol). Culpeper went so far as to declare that an ointment made with sanicle, scabious and bugle 'is so efficacious for all sorts of hurts in the body that none should be without it.'

Ajuga comes from the Latin *abigo*, meaning to drive away disease; *reptans*, 'creeping', which it does vigorously.

In Germany, if you pick bugle and bring the flowers indoors it was believed it would cause a fire

BUTTERCUP

Ranunculus species

'They grow common everywhere. Unless you run your Head into a hedge, you cannot but see them as you walk', commented Nicholas Culpeper. The buttercup's botanical name derives from *rana*, Greek for 'frog', since buttercups thrive in damp marshy places. The specific name *acris* means 'bitter', after the toxic protoanemonin contained in the plant. This is lost on drying, so buttercups can be harvested for hay, but it's noticeable that cows leave fresh buttercups alone in a meadow: although seldom fatal, eating them causes colic and inflammation of the intestinal membranes. It's not a brilliant pasture crop in any case, since *R. acris* secretes a substance that takes potassium out of the soil, inhibiting the growth of nitrogen-fixing bacteria and causing the more valuable clover to disappear while the buttercups become invasive.

Accordingly, my early Victorian edition of *The Language of Flowers* remarks that the buttercup is the most mischievous of any meadow flower, and stands for ingratitude. Handling the plant can inflame and blister the skin, and European beggars rubbed it into open sores to arouse the sympathy of passers-by. Pliny was the first to record this effect, recommending its use for removing leprous sores, and subsequently buttercups were used in country medicine to treat burns, sores and rheumatic pain.

'Enamel of gold' is how nature writer Richard Jefferies describes a buttercup meadow. Buttercups are much loved by children who hold a buttercup flower under each other's chin to get it to shine. The more it does, the more the owner of the chin loves butter, or will get rich, or is 'as good as gold'. Thomas Hardy describes this glow in *Tess of the d'Urbervilles*: 'As they crept along, stooping low to discern the plant, a soft yellow gleam was reflected from the buttercups into their shaded faces, giving them an elfish, moonlit aspect, though the sun was pouring upon their backs in all the strength of noon.' The sunshine trapped inside the flower actually increases the temperature deep inside it, attracting insect pollinators. The small heath and copper butterflies, and burnet, double square-spot, lunar yellow underwing and slender-striped rufous moths all nectar on buttercups.

Handling the plant can inflame and blister the skin, and European beggars rubbed it into open sores to arouse the sympathy of passers-by

The name 'buttercup' was rare before the eighteenth century; its more common name being crowfoot, the three-pronged shape of the leaf suggesting the feet of the sturdy corvid. The buttercup is a close relative of chalk-stream-loving water crowfoot that, as described by William Turner, 'swimmeth above the water in ponds for the most

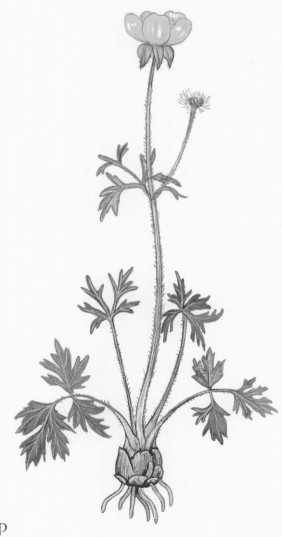

BULBOUS
BUTTERCUP
Ranunculus bulbosus

CREEPING
BUTTERCUP
Ranunculus repens

parte of the summer'. John Clare certainly knew it by this name: 'Gatherd a Crowflower in full bloom', he wrote in his *Journal* on New Year's Eve 1824, recording a rare instance of buttercups in midwinter.

In Ireland, cowherds used to rub buttercup flowers on cows' udders on May Day to increase their milk yield, and on Midsummer's Day cows were garlanded with buttercup chains to bless the milk, forging the 'butter' connection, which came from a fancied connection between the yellow of buttercups and the yellow of cream and butter from cows' milk. In folk medicine, buttercups were employed as a remedy for the king's evil, a tuberculosis of the lymph glands in the neck cured by the royal touch in days when people believed in the divine right of kings. It was also believed that buttercup roots ground up with suet cured the plague, by causing blisters that drew out the disease. A chain of buttercups hung around the neck cured lunacy – although conversely the smell of buttercups induced madness, one of its local names being crazy bet for this reason. However, to dream of buttercups meant a business enterprise would succeed.

> *In Ireland, cowherds used to rub buttercup flowers on cows' udders on May Day to increase their milk yield*

'Abundant are the sorts of this herb, that to describe them all would tire the patience of Socrates himself', sighed Culpeper. Cuckoo-bud, gilt cup, galland, yellow galland, butterflower, baffiners, bassinet, blister plant, butter cresses, carlock cups, clovewort, crowflower, eggs and butter, gil cup, horse gold, gold weed, butter daisy, mary buds and yellow cups are among the English names. The French know it as *bouton d'or*, the Germans as *Butterblume*.

BUTTERWORT

Pinguicula species

Glowing like sapphire gems on acid peaty soils, wet rocks and moorland, butterwort is essentially a northern plant, rarely seen on England's lowlands. It is carnivorous, the sticky leaves catching small insects or insects with large wings. Glands in the leaf produce enzymes which break down digestible components of the insect and provide the plant with food to make up for poor mineral nutrients in its habitat. Flowering from May to July, butterwort is pollinated by small bees.

In the Hebrides there's a tradition that if you pick butterwort it will protect you from witches, and if cows eat it they will be safe from the onslaught of elf-arrows. Rubbed on to the udders (as with buttercups), this plant will protect the milk and the butter. Since butterwort produces a bactericide, this application has been used by farmers to heal sores on their livestock. Gerard reported, 'the husbandmen's wives of Yorkshire do use to anoint the dugs of their kine with the fat an oilous juice of the herbe Butterwort, when they are bitten by venomous worm, or chapped, rifted, and hurt by any other meanes.' However, it was also blamed for sheep rot.

On a domestic level butterwort was used to curdle milk or thicken it to make a fermented buttermilk (Laplanders used it to curdle reindeer milk). Butterwort has found a use in orchid nurseries too, to combat insect pests. In folk medicine it was used as a vulnerary, and for treating ruptures. Being antispasmodic, it was prescribed in a remedy for chronic or convulsive coughs. Butterwort is also known as Yorkshire sanicle, bog violet and marsh violet. *Pinguis* means 'greasy', after the glistening leaves.

ALPINE BUTTERWORT
Pinguicula alpina

CAMPION

Red campion (Silene dioica)
White campion (Silene latifolia subsp. *alba)*
Bladder campion (Silene vulgaris)

Silene is the merry drunk of the woodlands, giving his mythological Greek name to the genus of wild flowers that establish themselves in woods and hedgerows all over Britain. It was the Romans though who gave campions their common name, weaving campion into garlands made to crown their champions at the public games in Rome. Later the flower became the 'champion' of English cottage gardens, producing the lovely magenta cultivar rose campion – *Silene coronaria* – now widely known as *Lychnis coronaria*.

The dark pink of the wild red campion's flower has attracted Robin-names, as well as that of Red Riding Hood. Various Devil-names allude to a superstition that, being a flower of the fairy folk, if you pick red campion someone in the family will die. Flowering from May to October along roadsides and in woodlands, bumblebees and butterflies nectar on it, and several moths feed on the foliage including the sandy carpet, rivulet and twin-spot carpet. In folk medicine, the crushed seeds of red campion were used to cure snakebites: its Welsh name *blodau neidr* means 'snake flower', and it has a West Country nickname of adder's flower. Its specific name *dioica* refers to the (scentless) flowers of a species that requires plants of separate sexes to make seeds. It is the flower of Saints Philip and James, the latter's Feast Day being 1 May.

White campion, found in open country, arable fields and wasteland, occasionally hybridises with the red to produce pink flowers. Also a snake flower, this too is a thunder plant and will provoke a storm if you pick it – or worse, strike you with lightning. Known as grave flower or flower of the dead, it's often found growing in churchyards near tombstones where moths flutter around it at night-time, attracted by its faint nocturnal scent.

With a local name of thunderbolt, in French *herbe du tonnerre*, bladder campion appears also to be a thunder flower – maybe to rural children the sound of its bloated calyx popping resembled a distant storm? Bumblebees are undeterred by the cavernous flower, whose nectar lies half an inch below the rims of the petals: where long-tongued bees and night moths may give up, bumblebees take a shortcut. They bite through the base of the flower and draw the nectar from the puncture – doing nothing in the process for pollination.

Bladder campion flowers emit a clove-like scent at evening, and the greenery has a pea-like flavour, which has won it a place in gastronomy: the young leaves and shoots are delicious in salads.

It was the Romans who gave campions their common name, weaving it into garlands made to crown their champions at the public games in Rome

In Italy, where bladder campion is known as *sciopentin*, the mature leaves are steamed or stir-fried with garlic and tossed into omelettes or into risottos. It is valued as a green vegetable in La Mancha in Spain, where it is known as *collejas*, traditionally added to a vegetable stew, added to a potato dish, or mixed with beans or rice. In Crete, where it is called *agriopapoula*, bunches of bladder campion leaves are sold in local shops and on markets, for serving sautéed in olive oil.

WHITE
CAMPION
Silene latifolia

BLADDER
CAMPION
Silene vulgaris

CENTAURY

Centaurium erythraea

The lovely centaury is a gentian, one of 1,600 species of the family *Gentianaceae*. Its star-shaped salmon-pink flowers bloom between June and September on grassland, along woodland borders and on road verges from the south coast to the Isle of Lewis, providing food for the dowdy plume moth. The genus was named after Chiron, the centaur legendary in Greek mythology for his skill in healing with medicinal herbs, who cured himself from a wound received from an arrow poisoned with the blood of the Hydra. Once regarded as a panacea, for all its healing and tonic properties centaury is extremely bitter: an old English name for the plant was felwort, after its ancient nickname fel terrae or gall of the earth (the related felwort or field wort *Gentianella amarella* is also a gentian). Of many bitter wild herbs, centaury is among the most effective, acting on the liver, spleen and kidneys, purifying the blood and acting as an excellent tonic. A stomachic, it helps digestion and stimulates the appetite. It is both antiseptic and febrifuge and came to be known as febrifuga and feverwort, for its use in bringing down a high temperature and even for treating malaria. Other names include filwort, red centaury, Christ's ladder – and steps of Christ since it was said to spring up at Calvary in Our Lord's footsteps.

Saxon herbalists used centaury for snake bites and other poisonings, as well as fevers. In a tenth-century poem there is mention of centaury as being powerful against 'wykked sperytis', an ancient magical herb with esoteric effects when mixed with (don't try this at home) the blood of a female lapwing or black-bellied plover. In more measured tones Culpeper tells us that 'the herbe is so safe that you cannot fail in the using of it, only give it inwardly for inward diseases, use it outwardly for outward diseases. Tis very wholesome, but not very toothsome.' He especially recommended centaury for dropsy, for eyesight, for wounds and ulcers, and other herbalists used it with barberry bark for jaundice. A decoction was used to eliminate body vermin such as head lice, and it was an effective vermifuge. Centaury formed the basis of the once famous Portland Powder, popularly taken for gout, and modern research confirms its potency in the treatment of rheumatism and gout: the plant contains the alkaloid gentianine, which has powerful anti-inflammatory properties.

Bach Flower Remedies include centaury as a remedy for people who find it difficult to say no: finding that others take advantage of their gentleness, the remedy acts to support self-determination and courage, to strengthen weak boundaries and to concentrate on their own paths in life. It is used by present-day herbalists for dyspepsia and heartburn, and for loss of appetite in anorexia. One of its local names, in common with red bartsia (*Odontites verna*) and yellow wort (*Blackstonia perfoliata*) is sanctuary, and the Irish consider it a blessed plant, bringing it into the house for good luck between the Annunciation on 25 March and the Assumption on 15 August.

CHAMOMILE

Matricaria recutita (German/wild)
Chamaemelum nobile syn. *Anthemis nobilis* (Roman/English)

'It hath floures wonderfully shynynge yellow and resemblynge the appell of an eye', is sixteenth-century botanist William Turner's cheerful description of Roman chamomile. To the Greeks it was 'earth apple' – *Chamaemelum* literally 'apple on the ground' – because of its fragrant apple-scent. There are many species of this daisy-like flower including the ubiquitous mayweed or Dog-daisy, annual weeds growing widely around arable fields and landfill sites: but only *Matricaria* (see p.65) and *Chamaemelum nobile* (illustrated above) have significant uses. The spelling 'camomile' corresponds to the Old French source for the name, whereas the more modern spelling 'chamomile' corresponds to the original Greek. *Nobile* refers to large flowers on a small plant. Corn chamomile (*Anthemis arvensis*) is food for the chamomile shark moth and *Phycitodes saxicola*.

The ancient Egyptians held chamomile in such reverence that they consecrated it to their deities, and it's been used in folk medicine ever since. The Saxons referred to it as one of the nine sacred herbs given to the world by Wotan. Today, chamomile tea is best known as a relaxant and a remedy for sleeplessness. But infusions of chamomile are also effective in purging intestinal worms, easing migraines and relieving stress. They are good for cramp, infantile colic, digestive-tract complaints and painful menstruation, and can be used externally as a poultice for skin conditions – soothing and effective in the bath for infant eczema for example. On analysis, it has been found to have anti-inflammatory, sedative, antispasmodic and cholesterol-lowering effects, and is prescribed in homeopathy for inner turmoil.

> *The ancient Egyptians held chamomile in such reverence that they consecrated it to their deities*

'The virtue of the herb is thus', claims Banckes's *Herball* of 1525, the first book printed in England that can really be called an herbal: 'If it be drunken with wine, it will break the stone. Also it destroyeth the yellow evil. It helpeth the aching and disease of the liver. It is good for the aching of a man's head and for the megrim.' Gerard's *Herbal* of 1597 claims that it is a tonic for fatigue as well. 'These plants are set in gardens both for pleasure and also profit. The oyle compounded of the floures performeth the same, and is a remedy against all wearisomeness, and is with good success mixed with all those things that are applied to mitigate pain.' Recent research in Germany indicates that chamomile is a wound–healer in animals and can be of benefit in animal diabetes.

Chamomile water acquired magical properties: an infusion sprinkled around the house will remove any curses put on it. Merely washing your hands in it will attract money and win you a bet.

Add chamomile to bath water, and love will come your way. William Turner declared, 'It will restore a man to hys color shortly yf a man after large use of the bathe drynke of yt after he come out of the bathe.'

Merely washing your hands in it will attract money and win you a bet

Lawn chamomile is still planted in formal gardens for the aroma that wafts up when trodden. It's an excellent companion: if it is grown near sickly plants they quickly recover, and healthy ones thrive next to it. The 'oyle' that Gerard mentions comes from both the wild chamomile and the Roman or Lawn chamomile. This blue essential oil, chamazulene, is extracted from the fresh flowers for its anti-inflammatory properties. *Matrix* is Latin for womb, from the use to which wild chamomile (*Matricaria*) was put to treat female conditions – but so potent is it that pregnant and nursing mothers are advised to avoid taking chamomile.

Chamomile oil makes an effective hair rinse for highlighting fair hair, and when massaged into the scalp gives lustre to lifeless hair. The plant produces a yellow dye and the whole herb was once used in the manufacture of beer. The light Spanish sherry Manzanilla ('little apple') is flavoured with chamomile. A traditional high-end tip for those who aspire to gracious living is to put chamomile water and orange peel into fingerbowls at table.

CORN
CHAMOMILE
Anthemis arvensis

YELLOW CHAMOMILE
Anthemis tinctoria

STINKING
MAYWEED
Anthemis cotula

SCENTED MAYWEED
Matricaria recutita

CHICKWEED

Stellaria media

Chickweed actually is weed for chicks, fed to chickens and goslings, as evidenced by local names of chickenweed, chickenwort and chicken's meat. It gets another name, passerina, after passerines or perching birds, because it was also fed to caged songbirds: Gerard tells us, 'little birdes in cages' are refreshed with it 'when they loath their meate'. In France chickweed is *herbe à l'oiseau*, in early Latin *Morsus gallinae* meaning 'hen's morsel'. Before the days of chemical herbicides, chickweed provided important nourishment for ground beetles and many of our farmland birds such as chaffinches, greenfinches and other seed-eaters. The plant is astonishingly prolific, self-pollinating with a life cycle of five to six weeks, setting seed and flower throughout the year (one of its local names is winterweed), and producing on average 2,500 seeds per plant (this can rise to 25,000). They are dispersed by ants and by birds through their droppings. Chickweed is an important food plant for several *Lepidoptera* including the beautiful chickweed geometer (*Haematopis grataria*), the satin wave, the lunar yellow and the plain clay.

Growing almost anywhere – in gardens, hedgerows, on disturbed ground, along field edges – it's one of our commonest weed and one of the most useful. Chickweed has always been an important medicinal herb, particularly for skin conditions, since its saponins soothe itching, and the juice of the plant or a poultice of the fresh leaves, or a manufactured ointment or cream, bring immediate relief. You can effectively treat inflammations, itchiness and rashes, as well as chronic eczema by hanging a bunch of the leaves in a muslin bag under the hot tap as it runs into the bath. Boils, abscesses and ganglia can be cured with it, and Dioscorides recommended it in an effective eye lotion. Some herbalists in the past claimed that chickweed water was a good remedy for obesity, 'to comfort troubled stomachs or to slim fat citizens'. This is an example of how country wisdom is more than whimsy: chickweed's saponins inhibit intestinal absorption of dietary fats and carbohydrates, and it is used in obesity treatments today.

> *Chickweed can produce up to 25,000 seeds per plant*

Fortunate are those who are prescribed it in a slimming diet: chickweed is a delicious green vegetable with a cress-like flavour, and bundles of it used to be sold on city streets. Its tender, soft leaves can be harvested year round to put in salads and sandwiches. It can also be steamed and eaten like spinach, or you can make a pesto sauce with it instead of using basil. It's highly nutritious, especially rich in copper and potassium, in phosphorus and iron as well as vitamins A and C. The Japanese, who use many wild foods in their cuisine, feature chickweed in their springtime festival Nanakusa-no-sekku.

The white starry flowers open early in the morning, and at night the surrounding leaves fold over to protect young buds and shoots. Chickweed opens its leaves fully to the sky if fine weather is to follow, but 'if it should be shut up', according to one Victorian writer, 'then the traveller is to put on his greatcoat'. The generic name *Stellaria* refers to the star-shaped flower, and *media* distinguishes its smaller size from its relatives the stitchworts and starworts.

COMMON MOUSE-EAR
Cerastium fontanum

FIELD MOUSE-EAR
Cerastium arvense

CINQUEFOIL

Potentilla species

A powerful plant this, flower of supernatural magic: in the Middle
Ages cinquefoil was an herb of divination, powerful against witches,
often hung over doorways in May Day garlands to keep them away.
It also came to denote distinction, the cinquefoil emblem of strength,
power and loyalty first appearing in eleventh-century Burgundian
church architecture, and featuring in the tracery of Gothic
stonemasons and wood carvers through to the sixteenth century.
Cinquefoil's five leaflets (*cinq feuilles*) represent the five senses of man,
depicted in heraldic devices to bequeath honour and distinction on
the man who masters his self. As such it appears on the coat of arms
of Bardolph of Bretagne who in 1066 was master of William the
Conqueror's military engineers corps.

The cinquefoil family is one of creeping perennials, which includes the barren strawberry (*P. sterilis*), tormentil (*P. erecta*) and silverweed (*P. anserina*), as well as the hoary (*P. argentea*), creeping (*P. reptans*) and trailing (*P. angelica*) cinquefoils. Silverweed was an important crop plant until the introduction of the potato in the sixteenth century. Its starchy root with a turnip flavour was eaten boiled or baked, or ground up to make bread and porridge – and for this reason cinquefoil acquired local names of bread and butter, and bread and cheese. One particularly weird snippet of folklore claims that medieval fishermen would fix cinquefoil to their nets to increase their catch of fish.

One particularly weird snippet of folklore claims that medieval fishermen would fix cinquefoil to their nets to increase their catch of fish.

In his poem *Love in the Valley*, George Meredith describes grassy glades as 'yellow with cinquefoil of the dew-grey leaf'. When it rains, the plant's silver-grey leaves curl up and bend over the yellow flower, forming a tent to protect the flower from the wet, a habit which led to the language of flowers giving it the attribute of 'beloved daughter'.

The generic name *Potentilla* derives from the medicinal potency of cinquefoil, recognised by Theophrastus in Ancient Greece. Traditionally, an herbal decoction from the roots cured fevers, and was used to treat malaria. The leaves are rich in iron, calcium and magnesium, and a gargle was made to cure mouth sores. Cinquefoil's analgesic properties alleviated acute pain, and the rustic lore of *The Countrie Farme* of 1616 recommended the powder or decoction of tormentil roots 'to appease the rage and torment of the teeth'. As an astringent it was used to stop bleeding, and a poultice would stop nosebleeds. An herbal or root tea was traditionally used to treat diarrhoea and even dysentery. To this day *P. erecta* or tormentil is still known in Scotland for treating stomach problems and digestive troubles. The seventeenth-century dramatist John Fletcher went further:

> This tormentil, whose vertue is to part
> All deadly killing poison from the heart.

One of cinquefoil's local names is blood root, since it contains the red dye tormentole, used in the past to colour leather and cloth. The plant's high tannin content led to its use instead of oak bark for tanning leather. The golden yellow buttercup-like flowers attract pollinating insects, and are visited by butterflies including the rare Karner blue. The leaves of certain species are eaten by grizzled skipper caterpillars, and are the food plant of the lunar yellow underwing, sword grass and annulet moths. Common names for cinquefoil include biscuits, five-fingers, five-leaf, flesh-and-blood and shepherd's knot.

MARSH CINQUEFOIL
Potentilla palustris

CLOVER

Trifolium pratense, T.repens and *T.hybridum*

W hen St Patrick arrived in Ireland to convert the Irish to Christianity in the sixth century, he was given permission to speak before the king. He found some difficulty in explaining the concept of the Trinity. Bending down, he picked a three-leaved clover and said, 'Look! Here are three leaves in one leaf!' The king, convinced, was converted. The shape of clover's three-lobed leaf is much used in church architecture, in window lights and tracery carved to represent the Trinity, and the plant itself used to be an integral part of floral decorations for Trinity Sunday. A dove, symbolic of the Holy Spirit, is sometimes depicted within the outlined form of a trefoil combined with a triangle. In Ireland, the trefoil or shamrock was adopted as the form of the Celtic cross, and became the national emblem. Ever since 1651, the shamrock has been worn on St

Patrick's day, 17 March, which also celebrates the close of winter, so clover came to symbolise summer.

Clover is a magical and protective plant, and North Country farmers put it in their stables to protect livestock. They say clover grows only where elves live, and that they give it its powers. It was a charm against witches and evil spirits as far back as the Druids, who venerated it:

> *Trefoil, Johnswort, Vervain and Dill*
> *Hinder the witches from their will.*

It's the only plant that will enable the wearer to see fairies, a floral talisman to open human eyes to the secrets of the fairy world. The lucky four-leaved clover, renowned for its powers, is the particular herb of the fairies:

> *I'll seek a four-leaved clover*
> *In all the fairy dells*
> *And if I find the charmed leaf*
> *O how I'll weave my spells.*

Place a four-leaved clover in the shoes of a traveller and he'll return safely to the arms of his lover. Put a four-leaved clover under your pillow and you will dream of your true love. The possession of a four-leafed clover will enable you to discover the identity of anyone practising witchcraft against you. And:

> *if you find an even ash or four-leaved clover,*
> *You'll be bound to see your true love ere the day be over.*

The plant became an emblem of hope and good luck after a legend that Eve was clutching a four-leaved clover when she was exiled from the Garden of Eden, and subsequently Hope was depicted by the ancients as a child standing on tiptoe holding a clover flower in his hand. Some clover leaves have been found with even more than four lobes: a five-leaved clover brings fame, six money, and seven prosperity. A two-leaved clover was used by East Anglian youngsters as a charm to discover the name of their future spouses:

> *A Clover, a Clover of two,*
> *Put it on your right shoe;*
> *The first young man or woman you meet*
> *In field, street or lane,*
> *You'll have him or one of his name.*

To dream of clover means health, happiness in marriage and, for a man, a prosperous wife. Clover is a weather-indicator too: if the leaves fold up, it means rain is on the way.

'Living in clover' is an epithet for a life of contentment and plenty, symbolised by fattened cattle browsing in clover-filled meadows. In the language of flowers clover stands for fertility, since the plant captures nitrogen from the air and releases nitrates into the soil. In addition, its high sodium content keeps grass rich and green. First cultivated in England in 1645, clover had previously been grown in Holland where farmers had long recognised its value as a crop, ploughed back into the soil to enrich it. Clover spreads very rapidly and can also lie dormant for many years before springing back to life. The flowers are pollinated by bumblebees, and honey bees are also eager collectors of the nectar, earning clover the name of bee bread. Clover is the food plant of the clouded yellow butterfly, red clover for the mazarine blue and the short-tailed blue, and white clover for the common and short-tailed blue. Around fifteen moths visit red clover, including the clover case-

> *They say clover grows only where elves live, and that they give it its powers*

74

bearer, the narrow-bordered five-spot burnet, the black rustic and the pearly underwing.

In herbal medicine Gerard says that, pounded with a little honey, clover 'takes away the pin and web in the eies, ceasing the pain and inflammation thereof if it be strained and dropped therein'. Red-clover syrup was a country cure for whooping cough, and an extract from the flowers used to treat sores. Red-clover wine was traditionally a blood and skin cleanser, and its hormone regulating effects used for treating breast cancer. Poultices made from the flower-heads could be applied to cancerous sores. The flowers and leaves make a gentle infusion for coughs and indigestion, acne, eczema, psoriasis, enlarged glands and treating the menopause, as well as being an effective sedative. The flowers are also a tasty and pretty addition to salads.

The name 'clover' comes from the Latin *clava*, 'a club', the three-knotted club of Hercules and the club of our playing cards. As the trefoil or shamrock it appears widely in heraldry. Various place-names derive from it, including Clavering and Claverton. *Trifolium* means 'three leaves'. Red clover's specific name *pratense* means 'of the meadows', while *repens*, 'of the white clover', means 'creeping': one the habitat, the other the habit. Culpeper wrote, 'It is so well known especially by the name of honeysuckles, white and red, that I need not describe them. They grow almost everywhere in this land.'

ALSIKE CLOVER
Trifolium hybridum

COLTSFOOT

Tussilago farfara

The butter-yellow flower of coltsfoot is also known as son before father because it appears in early spring, the leaves following later in the summer. In his 1597 *Herbal* Gerard points out that it could just as appropriately be called coughwort, and one of its common names is actually coughweed. For more than two millennia coltsfoot tea has been used to cure lung complaints and respiratory disorders. Coltsfoot lozenges were widely used as cough sweets, and the flower is still used today in Chinese herbal treatments for chest complaints. The leaves were put into herbal tobacco and smoked for bronchitis, asthma and chronic coughs, hence local names of baccy plant and poor man's baccy. The first-century Greek physician Dioscorides recommended it for dry coughs, and 'for those who are unable to breathe except standing upright'. The powdered leaves make herbal snuff for clearing the nasal passages and curing headaches. Coltsfoot leaves retain a place in the *British Pharmacopoeia*: rich in flavonoids, tannins, mucilage, zinc and vitamin C, coltsfoot never fails as a cough remedy, and extracts of the whole plant have been shown to increase immune resistance. However, coltsfoot contains liver-toxic pyrrolizidine alkaloids, so all manufactured remedies are now made from alkaloid-free cultivars, and are particularly effective when mixed with wild cherry.

Coltsfoot became a favourite with apothecaries who painted its sunburst-yellow flowers on their shop signs, since they regarded it as a cure-all. A decoction of the leaves soothed insect bites and burns, cured ulcers and reduced swellings. A lotion of coltsfoot would heal cuts, and bruised leaves applied to wounds would hasten their recovery. Pliny recommended a recipe for a feeling of well-being: burn the leaves on a fire of cypress woodand inhale the fumes, sipping wine between each puff. The plant had non-medicinal uses too: the soft down from the underside of the leaves was dipped into a solution of saltpetre for tinder boxes, and used to kindle a fire. The fresh leaves, rich in vitamin C, can be chopped into salads, and the flowers were used in country wine-making. Coltsfoot leaves give a yellow dye, and goldfinches line their nests with the down from the seedheads, which appear in spring.

> *Coltsfoot became a favourite with apothecaries who painted its sunburst-yellow flowers on their shop signs, since it was regarded as a cure-all*

A plant of roadsides, banks and cliffs, verges and waste ground, coltsfoot is native to Europe. The flowers, which close up at night and in dull weather, attract bees and hoverflies. Coltsfoot is the food plant for half a dozen moths including the triangle plume. William Coles, in his *The Knowledge of Plants*, maintained 'if the down flieth off colt's foot, dandelion and thistles when there is no wind, it is a sign of rain'.

Also known as tushalagies, yellow stars, foalfoot, clatterclogs and hoofs, coltsfoot gets its name from the hoof-like shape of the leaf.

The generic Latin comes from *tussis ago*, 'I drive away a cough', reflected in a Scottish nickname tushylucky. The specific name *farfara* derives from two Latin words meaning 'mealy,' and 'to bear', with reference to the mealy white appearance of the stems and the downy undersides of the leaves.

ALPINE COLTSFOOT
Homogyne alpina

COMFREY

Symphytum officinale

Comfrey has been valued in herbal medicine since the first century AD, when Dioscorides gave it the botanical name of *Symphytum*, 'growing together'. Pliny alludes to it as *Conferva*: 'the roots be so glutinative that they will solder or glew together meat that is chopt in pieces, seething in a pot, and make it into one lump: the same bruysed and layd in the manner of a plaister, doth heale all fresh and green wounds.' Comfrey was introduced into England as a medicinal plant by knights returning from the Crusades, who used it to heal battlefield wounds. Thereafter monks grew it in physic gardens as a wound-healer and bone-setter, and the seed was sold by early nurserymen for medicinal purposes, acquiring for the herb the classification of *officinale*.

There was more to discover. Comfrey has been found to contain the alkaloid allantoin, which repairs and replaces cells of damaged connective tissue, from digestive ulcers to ulcerating wounds. Demulcent, astringent and anti-inflammatory, comfrey increases the rate at which the body heals injuries, including speeding the repair of ligament and tendon injuries. For broken bones, the turnip-like roots are lifted in spring, grated and powdered, used like plaster of Paris, and spread on gauze before laying on the affected part.

Comfrey became a common cottage-garden plant, grown by country housewives for the home's medicine cabinet. They crushed the dried leaves into tablets, and used juice from the root mixed with sugar and liquorice to cure coughs, or to make a tea prescribed for chest ailments. A general tonic and reviver of 'downcast spirits', this infusion could also be applied to bruises, burns, acne, boils, strains and sprains, and arthritis. Gerard claimed it should be 'given to drinke against the paine of the backe, gotten by violent motion as wrestling or overmuch use of women'.

Comfrey contains large amounts of vitamin B12, the only land plant known to contain it, and was therefore a valuable source of food for vegans – although comfrey root has been found to contain pyrrolizidine alkaloids that can cause liver damage and may be carcinogenic in large doses. So it is for external use only: a poultice prepared with the fresh leaves can effectively reduce swellings and sprains, expedite bone repair, and heal cuts and wounds. Comfrey ointment is effective for skin complaints and insect bites, and the stings of bees, horseflies and wasps.

Comfrey is related to borage, and like all members of the same family has hairy stalks and long rough leaves. 'The floures be round and hollow like little bells' is sixteenth-century botanist Henry Lyte's

> *Comfrey was introduced into England as a medicinal plant by knights returning from the Crusades, who used it to heal battlefield wounds*

description of the drooping clusters of cream or blue-purple bugles appearing from May to June. It flourishes in the moist soils of low-lying land all over the British Isles, often on riverbanks and alongside wet ditches, streams and ponds. Insect-pollinated, comfrey is a vigorous and fast-growing perennial that likes shade and damp, and is hard to eradicate once it gets going. It's a great plant for composting though, so if it runs riot in the garden put it in your heap to add nitrogen and to accelerate decomposition. You can make excellent green manure by soaking a bagful of comfrey leaves in a bucket of rainwater for a few days before straining them off and using them as a potassium-rich plant fertiliser.

It was first called 'comfrey' in England by William Turner in 1538, the name deriving from *confirmare*, 'to knit together' (broken bones), or *confervere*, 'to grow together'. Or it may derive from being a 'comforte to the joynctis' – 'comfrey' as a fifteenth century variation on the word 'comfort'. Common names include knit-bone, knit-back, bone set, nip-bone, ass-ear, bruisewort, gooseberry pie, pigweed, blackwort, consolida and consound (a generic term for plants used by herbalists for medicinal purposes). In French it is *consoude* or *oreille d'âne* ('donkey's ears' from the shape and floppiness of the leaves), in German *Wallwurz* meaning 'wall-root'. In Lincolnshire it's known as Abraham, Isaac or Jacob, from the colour range of comfrey flowers from white to pink to purple to blue.

TUBEROUS COMFREY
Symphytum tuberosum

CONVOLVULUS

Convolvulus arvensis

B ane of the gardener's life but closely related to the lovely
morning glory of poets and lovers, it's hard to dismiss
convolvulus as nothing but a pest since its flowers are so
gorgeous. They featured in garlands in ancient Greece and Rome,
and the seventeenth-century herbalist, gardener and botanist John
Parkinson recommended them on trellis work and verandahs as a
graceful bower-flower. George Gissing, in *The Private Papers of Henry
Ryecroft*, wrote 'Nearby is a hedge covered with the great white
blossoms of the bindweed. My eyes do not soon grow weary'.

The ninth Aztec emperor Montezuma grew a species of
convolvulus in his Mexican palace gardens in the early sixteenth
century (probably the psychedelic morning glory *Rivea corymbosa*), and
one of his specimens was said to have climbed to the incredible height

of 6,000 feet in six months. An annual or perennial vine belonging to a genus of between 100–150 species, convolvulus will easily swamp plants growing nearby, but is a valuable food plant for several *Lepidoptera* including the sweet potato leaf miner, the gem, the white plume and common plume moths. *Convolvo* means 'I intertwine', as in a lover's embrace – but with a darker side, as suggested by one of *C. arvensis's* commonest names, bindweed. In the language of flowers pink convolvulus represents love sustained, but also obstinacy. Cornbine and devil's guts it has been called too, by those in rage or despair at failing to remove the persistent roots by fair means or foul, since convolvulus defies all but industrial-strength weedkillers.

Its relative morning glory, found to have hallucinogenic properties, is famed worldwide for its beauty. Let the poet have the last word here, 'infinity in a few strokes' according to its translator:

> *The morning glory climbs above my head,*
> *Pale flowers of white and purple, blue and red.*
> *I am disquieted.*
> *Down in the withered grass something stirred;*
> *I thought it was his footfall that I heard.*
> *Then a grasshopper chirred.*
> *I climbed the hill just as the new moon showed*
> *I saw him coming on the southern road.*
> *My heart lays down its load.*

FROM 'LYRICS FROM THE CHINESE', A 3,000-YEAR-OLD SONG
TRANSLATED BY HELEN WADDELL

CORNFLOWER

Centaurea cyanus

Although Ceres, Greek goddess of the harvest of the cornfields, wore a cornflower in her hair, the stunning blue of the cornflower has all but disappeared from Britain's farmland, along with the meadows that are its wild habitat. This annual weed of intense sapphire blue has been virtually eradicated in arable fields by herbicides, depriving the *Sitochroa verticalis* moth of its food plant. Cornflowers are now more likely to be found growing in gardens, or in florists' polytunnels. In the wild, they flower (or used to) from May through to August, growing easily in well-drained, sunny fields, and the flowers can be added to summer salads. The petals are considered to have tonic, stimulant and emmenagogue properties, and dried cornflowers are sometimes an ingredient of Earl Grey tea.

A weird and wonderful nugget of country lore goes that if you have a nosebleed on the moveable summer Feast of Corpus Christi, hold cornflowers in your hand until they are warm, and your nosebleed will stop. In herbal medicine, cornflowers were first mentioned by Hildegard von Bingen, and the plant has been found to contain cninin which is antibiotic. The deep blue colour of the flowers came to symbolise eyes, and an infusion of the flower petals was used as an eyewash for treating conjunctivitis and tired eyes (cornflower for blue eyes, plantain for brown). This is still used in herbal medicine in France today, where they also prescribe the petals as a poultice. A cornflower floral water is distilled to make an astringent and antiseptic skin-toner, and an infusion can be used as a mouthwash. The seeds are a safe mild laxative for children.

Remains of cornflowers were found in the funeral wreath made for Tutankhamen, who was young when he died, and fresh cornflowers came to be worn by young men in love: if the flower faded too quickly, it was taken as a sign that his love was not returned. It's a flower for mopers, prompting authors such as the nineteenth-century German novelist Theodor Fontane to satirise it, and the moping lovers.

> *Remains of cornflowers were found in the funeral wreath made for Tutankhamen*

The blue cornflower became one of the national flowers of Germany. There's a story that when Queen Louise of Prussia was fleeing Berlin pursued by Napoleon's forces, she hid her children in a field of cornflowers and kept them quiet by getting them to weave wreaths from the flowers. The cornflower became identified with Prussia, giving its colour to the Prussian military uniform. Prussian blue gave its name to prussic acid (hydrogen cyanide) or 'blue acid', and the word cyanide comes from the Greek *kyanos*, blue, hence the derivation of the cornflower's botanical genus. Cyanus was a Greek poet who sang of the beauties of the earth. He worshipped Chloris (known as Flora to the Romans) and spent his time gathering flowers for her altar. When he died the goddess turned him into a cornflower.

Having grown on Estonian soil for more than ten thousand years, commonly in rye fields, the cornflower symbolises daily bread to the Estonians and since 1968 has been their national flower. It was the favourite flower of J. F. Kennedy and was worn by his son John F. Kennedy Junior at his own wedding in tribute to his deceased father. In France the *bleuet de France*, an emblematic cornflower, is the symbol of the First World War Armistice.

Centaurea comes from the same derivation as the flower centaury, although in this case it's because the centaur Chiron used cornflower petals to cure a wound made by an arrow dipped in the Hydra's blood. John Clare describes cornflowers as 'blue caps in the wheat', the common country name bluebottle derives from a time when cornflower petals were pressed for making ink, and could certainly have been one of the wild flowers that prompted him to write, 'I grew so much into the quiet love of nature's presence that I was never easy but when I was in the fields.' *Centaurea cyanus* is also known locally as bachelor's button, bluecup, blue blobs, blue bonnets, cornbottle, boutonniere flower, hurtsickle – and gogglebuster: prepare to be dazzled – or for your spectacles to be broken, because in French cornflowers are *casse-lunette*.

COWSLIP

Primula veris

And I serve the Fairy Queen
To dew her drops upon the green:
The cowslips tall her pensioners be;
In their gold coats spots you see;
These be rubies, fairy favours:
In those freckles live their savours.

SHAKESPEARE, *A MIDSUMMER NIGHT'S DREAM*

A northern European legend has it that the cowslip is the herb of St Peter and the keys of heaven. When St Peter learned that a duplicate set had been forged, and that some souls were entering through a back door, he was so shocked he dropped his keys to earth. Up sprang the first cowslip, with flower-heads resembling a bunch of keys. More prosaically, cowplop, cooslop and cowslop tell us that the cowslip flourishes on well-manured pastureland, and John Clare called it cowslap, noting 'this is a very favourite flower with us among all classes'. The Anglo-Saxons called it 'cuslippe' because to them it smelled like cows' breath. Growing widely in established meadows, on hedgerows and in clearings, cowslips are rarer in the north, and there's the occasional phenomenon of a double cowslip: Gerard refers to and illustrates one as 'Two in a Hose', and in *A Garden of Pleasant Flowers* (originally published in 1629) John Parkinson describes 'Double cowslips one within another, or Hose in Hose. The only difference of this kinde from the ordinary field Cowslip is, that it beareth one single flower out of another.'

Cowslips are also fairy cups, fairies' flowers, milk-maidens and freckled faces because the fine crimson spots in the throat of the flower are said to have magical powers to restore youthful bloom and beauty. The sixteenth-century naturalist William Turner was scathing about such cosmetic uses: 'Some women we find, sprinkle ye floures of cowslip wt whyte wine and after still it and wash their faces wt that water to drive wrinkles away and to make them fayre in the eyes of the worlds rather than in the eyes of God, whom they are not afraid to offend.'

The fine crimson spots in the throat of the flower are said to have magical powers to restore youthful bloom and beauty

In his *Herbal* of 1597 Gerard called cowslips Palsywort, since they were used in medieval folk medicine to cure palsy and paralysis – by association, shaking flower-heads for shaking limbs. One early herbalist made excessive claims on its behalf: 'That of Cowslips doth marvellously strengthen the Braine, preserveth against Madnesse, against the decay of memory, stoppeth headache and most infirmities thereof'. Could it really cure, as Gerard claims, 'vertigo, false apparitions, phrenzies, falling sickness, palsies, convulsions, cramps and all the diseases of the sinews'?

More credibly, a few handfuls of cowslips in a warm bath are said to relieve fatigue. Made into wine, or dried and used like a hop-pillow, they help insomnia and even, so they say, amnesia. Containing saponins, flavonoids and tannins, cowslips are antioxidant, anti-inflammatory and antispasmodic. The flowers are sedative and have proved effective in calming overactive children and in treating asthma. The root is expectorant and clears phlegm, being good for chronic coughs, bronchitis and catarrh. John Clare remembers 'Gathering Cows lips for wine': worth trying this (or the tea) as a cure for migraine or jangled nerves, if nothing else works. And carry a cowslip to bring good luck, or even to preserve youthfulness.

There used to be a rural pastime of making cowslip-balls or tisty tosties. Playing catch with a ball made of the closely-packed flowers, young girls would chant,

> *Cowslip ball, tell me true*
> *Who shall I be married to?*

According to the Victorian chronicler of folklore Richard Folkard, 'The umbels or heads are picked as close as possible to the top of the main stalks. From fifty to sixty of these are hung across a string stretched between the backs of two chairs. The flowers are then pressed carefully together, and the string tied tightly so as to collect them into a ball.' Each of the girls in turn would call out the names of eligible bachelors in the village, and if one of them dropped the ball, the last named would be the lad she would marry. John Clare was familiar with this game: writing from the Northampton Asylum where he spent the last twenty-two years of his life, he reminisced in a poem called 'Cowslips':

For they want some for tea and some for wine
And some to make a 'cuckaball'
To throw across the garlands silken line
That reaches o'er the street from wall to wall.

The cowslip is the food plant of the Duke of Burgundy butterfly, as well as the lunar yellow underwing and plain clay moths. Country people believed that it was the favourite flower of the nightingale, saying that it sings only where the cowslip is to be found in abundance. John Clare recalls going to a much-loved haunt one March day: 'I went to Lolham brigs to fish & there was an old croney at work the consequence was the joining for a bottle of ale which we sat & drank in the field under the wall of one of the brigs as we warmd with our beer he reflectd on the age of the brigs & remarkd what scores had past over them that was now in the dust [he] pointed to sprouting cowslips as a promise of spring &c his observations struck me so forcibly that I could not get it out of my head...'

A bank of cowslips is a springtime idyll, and certainly Izaak Walton thought so when putting the world to rights in *The Compleat Angler*: 'When the lawyer is swallowed up in business, and the statesman is preventing or contriving plots, then we sit on cowslip banks, hear the birds sing, and possess ourselves in as much quietness as these silent silver streams which we see glide so quietly by us'.

OXLIPS AND PAIGLES

The hybrid *P. veris* x *vulgaris* is described by Geoffrey Grigson in *The Englishman's Flora* as a 'coarse hybrid between Primrose and Cowslip, which lacks the charm of either parent, or of the woodland oxlip, or Paigle, of the eastern counties, *Primula elatior*. Such names as oxlip, Bedlam cowslip, or bullslop show how the difference was felt'. He has a point about the hybrid, which is showy and blousy, and right about the charm of the oxlip. *P. elatior* is one of the jewels of ancient woodland, palest yellow, a flower of grace and to my eye even more beautiful than the cowslip. It is the food plant of the square-spotted clay moth.

OXLIP
Primula elatior

DAISY

Bellis perennis

That of all the floures in the mede,
Than love I most thise floures white and rede,
Suche as man callen daysyes in our toun,
To hem have I so gret affecioun.

Geoffrey Chaucer, Prologue 'The Legend of Good Women'

The 'day's eye', Chaucer's beloved flower, was a 'blissful sight that softeneth al my sorwe'. To him it was innocent and pure, 'Eie of the Daie, emperice and flour of floures alle', with golden centre and emanating rays, *solis oculus*, eye of the sun. Centuries later he might have enjoyed the usually serious-minded Alfred Lord Tennyson's prank: 'He declared that he had persuaded one charming town-bred lady, to whom he was much attached, that a common daisy was a peculiar rhododendron only found on the Isle of Wight.'

Daisies came to represent Mary's tears when she pricked her finger while picking daisies to give to baby Jesus. A little blood smeared on to the petals, giving them a pink tinge. *Marienblümchen* became a symbol of innocence, and also of fidelity, and was adopted as such by crusading knights. In France the common daisy is *pâquerette* because it starts flowering around Easter (*Pâques*), and ox-eye daisy is herb Margaret or *Marguerite*, after the thirteenth-century saint Margaret of Cortona, a penitent of the Third Order of St Francis.

Bellis perennis means beautiful forever, and children (usually female) love to make daisy chains:

Girls who wear a daisy chain
Grow up pretty, never plain.

It is the flower of the newborn, in some places called bairnwort, in the belief that a daisy chain would protect an infant from being carried away by the fairies. For generations young girls have played 'He loves me, he loves me not', taking off one petal at a time to find the answer.

Daisy flowers close at night and during rainy weather, and spring has not sprung until you can put your foot on twelve daises (evidently spring comes earlier to those with big feet). If you don't put your foot on the first daisy you see in spring, then daisies will be sure to grow over you or one of your loved ones before the year is out. It's lucky to dream of daisies in spring or summer, but unlucky in autumn or winter, and country girls put daisies under their pillows to dream of their lovers.

To herbalists, daisy was primarily a wound herb, suggested by word association with the generic *Bellis*, since *bellum* is Latin for war. In ancient Rome, surgeons who accompanied legions into battle would order their slaves to pick sacks full of daisies to help staunch bleeding wounds. They extracted the juice, soaked bandages in the liquid, and applied it to sword gashes and spear cuts. Daisy ointment was also applied to boils, varicose veins and bruises, on which it had a similar effect as arnica – hence a local name of bruisewort. Gypsies claimed that daisy water cured acne and eczema, even a red nose and red blotches on the face, and that chewing the leaves would help cure mouth ulcers.

Gerard says that 'juice put into the eies cleareth them', and that daisies will 'mitigate all kinde of paines, especially in the joints and gout, if they be stamped with unsalted butter', among other things. A mild decoction of the flowers may ease coughs, and is a diuretic. The leaves can be used as a culinary herb or added to salads. Dried daisies make a refreshing tonic bath, and the plant yields a pale green dye.

Local names include billy button, boneflower, cat-posy, dickey daisy and hens and chickens. In Germany, the daisy is gooseflower, since geese like to graze on it. The daisy, along with the primrose, triggered nostalgia in John Clare's old age: 'to others they are but white and yellow flowers but to me they speack of seasons gone & joys that never return'.

DANDELION

Taraxacum officinale

Tis May and yet the March flower dandelion
Is still in bloom among the emerald grass
Shining like guineas with the suns warm eye on.
JOHN CLARE

The dandelion gets its name from *dent de lion*, although nobody is quite sure why. The tap-root is as white as a lion's tooth, the flower the same colour as the golden teeth of the heraldic lion or, the lion being the animal symbol of the sun, this is his flower shining golden rays in wild places. A fifteenth-century surgeon was so impressed with the medicinal powers of the dandelion that he said it was as strong and powerful as a lion's tooth. Certainly the saw-tooth leaves are jagged like a jawful of leonine teeth. Take your pick.

The dandelion is a rustic oracle, opening fully in sunny weather, and closing during rain. Clockflowers, fairy clocks, peasants' clock, old man's clock and time-flower are names that reflect this, as does a traditional ditty,

> Dandelion with globe of down
> The schoolboy's clock in every town,
> Which the truant puffs amain
> To conjure lost hours back again.

Dandelion seedheads are also a barometer: if they fly off when there is no wind, it means rain is coming. 'If the down flieth off Coltsfoot, dandelion and thistles when there is no wind, it is a sign of rain.' A youngster's oracle it is, too: if children blow all the seeds away while telling the time, their mother will not be calling them home, but if a few seeds remain, they should run home at once (but not before catching one on the wing and making a wish).

The dandelion is nature's great healer: a potent natural medicine recommended by Arab physicians in the eleventh century, it retains a place in the *British Pharmacopoeia*. Dandelions contain more vitamins B, C and pro-vitamin A than many vegetables or fruits, and are rich in proteins, sugar, fat, and numerous mineral salts including high levels of potassium. They contain calcium, silica and magnesium, sulphur, sodium, alkaloids and tannins. The root cleanses the liver, promoting bile for gall-bladder complaints. The bitter agents that stimulate the liver promote appetite and improve digestion. Dandelion's action on the kidneys is extremely diuretic, removing toxins from urine and flushing uric acid from the body, proving effective in treating gout and joint pain from rheumatism to arthritis and osteoarthritis. The diuretic effect also helps reduce high blood pressure. Dandelions are a purgative and mild laxative in cases of chronic constipation. By the Doctrine of Signatures the yellow dandelion is a cure for jaundice.

One of its most endearing names is monk's halo, after the pitted head with its translucent nimbus. On the other hand, it's Devil's milk plant, after the milky white sap in the stem. According to herbalists from Gerard onwards, warts and pimples are cured by applying this sap to the skin. Apparently, if you gather dandelion flowers on 23 June, eve of the feast of St John, they will repel witches. Dreaming of dandelions is an omen of misfortunes to come. In Ireland, dandelion is known as heart-fever grass, 'a sovereign remedy against swooning and passions of the heart'.

> *The dandelion is a rustic oracle, opening fully in sunny weather, and closing during rain*

The generic *Taraxacum* is medieval Latin derived from the Persian for 'bitter pot-herb', an edible plant. Young dandelion leaves are delicious in salads, with the added virtue, it is claimed, of improving the complexion and detoxifying the system. They can be blanched like chicory and eaten white. They contain more iron than spinach and more vitamin C than lettuce, and are a powerful diuretic – hence local names of Jack-piss-the-bed, pissy beds, tiddle-beds, wet-the-bed, and piss-a-bed. Conversely, an old wives' tale suggests that getting children to smell dandelions on May Day, 1 May, will inhibit bedwetting for a year! In French, dandelion is *pissenlit*, and there is a classic recipe for *pissenlit au lard* in which crisply fried strips of streaky bacon are mixed with croutons, and served on lettuce and young dandelion leaves tossed in olive oil.

Dandelion leaves are also used to brew beer, apparently once popular with steel workers. The flowers make a good country wine, and are delicious in their own right, the petals sprinkled on to spring salads. Dandelion coffee, made from the dried tap-roots, was popular during the Second World War when real coffee was at a premium. Dandelion tea can clear up skin blemishes, even eczema, and also relieve sore eyes. John Evelyn writes in his *Acetaria* of 1699 that 'The French country people eat the roots, and 'twas with this homely sallet the good wife Hecate entertained Theseus.'

Dandelions – of which there are two hundred micro-species – belong to the daisy family and are found almost everywhere worldwide, in grassy habitats, waste places, fields, gardens and roadsides. The bright yellow flowers open from grey-violet florets from late spring through to October, and the whole plant is visited by 93 species of insects and no fewer than 15 moths, including the satin wave, the pearly underwing, the small mottled willow and the stout dart.

Perhaps it's easy to be blasé about such a common weed: not so for Edward Thomas:

> *If they had reaped their dandelions and sold*
> *Them fairly, they could have afforded gold.*

Nor for Roger Deakin, who wittily coined 'a host of golden dandelions' in his journal.

DEADNETTLE

Lamium species

The white deadnettle, *Lamium album*, is known as Adam and Eve in the Bower because if you look deep inside the flowers, the golden and black stamens lying side by side look like two sleeping figures in a white silk bed – although the seventeenth-century simpler William Coles (a simpler is an herbalist who uses one herb at a time in treatments) saw it differently: 'The flower of the deadnettle is like a weasell's face.' Children would be shown how to ease the flower from the calyx and suck the sweet nectar out of the base, or how the hollow stem, square in cross-section, could be dried and made into a makeshift whistle. Local names of fairy boots and fairy feet describe the black stigmas cradled in the white lip of the flower, placed there by the fairies when they have finished dancing.

Deadnettles are hedgerow food, used as a culinary herb in Scandinavia where the young tops and leaves are lightly steamed and served with butter. They can be put into a stir-fry as a spring vegetable, or added to sauces, finely chopped. One of nature's gynaecological herbs, white deadnettle's astringent and demulcent properties make it a uterine tonic, which is effective in reducing menstrual flow, since its high tannin content stems the flow of blood. Its astringency makes it useful in cases of diarrhoea and leucorrhoea or vaginal discharge. White deadnettle tea sweetened with honey is a country cure for

'The flower of the deadnettle is like a weasell's face'

chills and colds. The flowers, boiled in water, have been used to cure catarrh and dropsy, and the roots boiled for kidney stones. Externally, it has been used on varicose veins.

Deadnettles grow in woodlands and waysides, on moist soils and in grassland, and their superficial likeness to the stinging nettle protects them from being eaten by rabbits and other herbivores, deterred by the similarity. Also called bee nettle, the flowers are attractive to bees as an early source of nectar and pollen. The nectar is available only to them because of their weight, lying so deep inside the narrow corolla that lighter insects cannot reach it. White deadnettle leaves provide food for slugs and snails, and all the deadnettles are food plants for larvae of a variety of *Lepidoptera* including the setaceous Hebrew character, the flame and gold spangle moths.

Red deadnettle, also known as purple archangel (*L. purpureum*) grows throughout the year and is also a bee plant. Henbit deadnettle (*L. amplexicaule*) looks very similar, but has stalk-less leaves. The beautiful *Lamiastrum galeobdolon* (syn. *L. luteum*), is our yellow archangel, which thrives in damp glades and makes a lovely garden shade plant with its glowing golden flowers. The flowers, tops and leaves can be made into tisanes, decoctions and tinctures and have been used for bladder paralysis in the elderly, and for general bladder problems and kidney complaints. Culpeper remarks, 'the yellow archangel is most commended for old, filthy, corrupt sores and ulcers, yea, although they grow to be hollow, and to dissolve tumours.'

Lamium means 'throat', from the enlarged throat of the corollas. *Album* is 'white', *luteum* 'gold', and *purpureum* 'red–purple'. *Galeobdolon* derives from the Greek *gale*, 'weasel', and *bdolo*, 'stench', from the acrid smell of the yellow archangel.

WHITE DEADNETTLE
Lamium album

SPOTTED DEADNETTLE
Lamium maculatum

ELECAMPANE

Inula helenium

Legend is undecided about *helenium*: either elecampane acquired its specific name because when Helen of Troy, Menelaus' wife, eloped with her lover Paris she had some in her hand: she made 'a goodly medecine of this herbe, agaynst the deadly Venome, or poyson of Serpentes' according to Bullein's *Booke of Simples* in 1562 (this is substantiated by Gerard, who declared 'It took the name Helenium of Helena, wife of Menelaus, who had her hands full of it when Paris stole her away into Phrygia'). Or, as Pliny would have it, elecampane sprang from the tears of Helen as she was wrested away from her lover by her jealous husband.

Elecampane is native to central Asia, introduced to Britain as a garden and medicinal plant by either the Celts or the Romans. It occasionally naturalises as an escape, and can be found in wild places in the UK, on waste ground, roadsides, in old meadows and orchards. Cultivated as a physic garden plant, it can still be found in meadows and old orchards, or growing in established cottage gardens (folklore

Recent research shows that extracts from the herb kill MRSA

decrees that growing it will attract fairies to the garden). It's worth having: *Enula campana reddit praecordia sana*, 'Elecampane will sustain your spirits', according to a Latin maxim. It grows to 6ft (150cm) tall from a thick branching root, flowering from July to August with large yellow, many-rayed flower-heads up to 3in (8cm) across, pollinated by bees and hoverflies.

In 1804 inulin, a bactericidal expectorant and tonic polysaccharide (the same as found in Jerusalem artichokes) was discovered in high levels (40 per cent) in the tubers of elecampane. Its mucilage soothes bronchial linings and is invaluable in chronic bronchitis and chest complaints. It is also a vermifuge, a tonic for the digestive system and used in dyspepsia. The tubers also contain helenin, a powerful antiseptic and bactericide, and recent research shows that extracts from the herb kill MRSA as well as a spectrum of other bacteria. In Chinese medicine elecampane is used for bronchial and breathing problems, and in the USA, where Amerindians used it for lung ailments, it is used for respiratory illness. Herbalists past and present prescribed it as an expectorant, a diuretic, and to bring on menstruation.

Yes, more; this little bottle of elecampane Will raise dead men to walk again

Both Pliny and Dioscorides considered elecampane good for coughs, and for centuries the plant was a traditional remedy for persistent catarrh, asthma and even whooping cough, as well as general bronchial complaints (Gerard prescribes it for 'the shortness of breath'). The Romans used it for indigestion and promoting appetite. To the Anglo-Saxons and Celts, it was sacred as well as medicinal, and by the seventeenth century elecampane was widely cultivated for its medicinal properties. Culpeper wrote that 'It groweth in moist grounds and shadowy places oftener than in the dry and open borders of field and lanes and other waste places, almost in every county in this country.'

Elecampane was taken either in decoction or as a piece of candied root with honey or sugar. Galen said 'it is good for passions of the hucklebone called sciatica'. Markham's *Countrie Farme* of 1616 said: 'The wine wherein the root of Elicampane hath steept is singularly good against the colicke.' Basically, elecampane could cure anything: venemous bites, plague, bad eyesight, intestinal parasites, period pain, heart conditions. A couplet quoted by Thomas Hardy in *The Return of the Native* goes further:

Yes, more; this little bottle of elecampane
Will raise dead men to walk again.

It's difficult to argue with an herb that works effectively on animals, because no placebo effect applies. Elecampane has proved its use in horse medicine, as per its common names of horshele, horshale or horseheal. It is used in veterinary medicine for equine skin diseases and for sheep affected with the scab, hence scabwort. It is still cultivated in continental Europe for medicinal use, mainly in Holland, Switzerland and in Germany. The roots, aromatic and with a warm, bitter taste, are used to flavour wines and liqueurs in central Europe, and are an ingredient of absinthe. They can also be (and often were) candied and eaten as a sweetmeat. A blue dye can be extracted from the root, with whortleberry.

Other local names include wild sunflower, elf docke, and *Marchalan* in Welsh. *The Grete Herball* of 1526 lists it as *Enula campana*, as from Campania in Italy.

EYEBRIGHT

Euphrasia species

The eyebrights range in colour from blue and white to pale
violet, sometimes with red or yellow markings on the lower
petal – which to believers in the Doctrine of Signatures (see
page 10) made it look like a bloodshot eye. A tiny annual of numerous
species, which hybridise easily, eyebright flowers from July to
September on short grassland. The plant is semi-parasitic, feeding off
the roots of grasses, which makes it useful in meadow management,
keeping vigorous grass at bay and allowing other wild flowers to
flourish. The larger varieties are pollinated by bees and hoverflies,
while the small ones self-pollinate. Eyebright is a food plant of the
pretty pinion and heath rivulet moths.

Eyebright's properties were originally recognised by Hildegard
von Bingen, but not until the sixteenth century did eyebright become

highly regarded by herbalists as a treatment for eye conditions. Gerard held that 'it preserveth the sight, increaseth it, and being feeble and lost restoreth the same'. It contains iridoid glycosides, notably aucubin, as well as tannins, which tighten the mucous membranes of the eye.

It's a popular herbal remedy in many countries, principally for eyestrain or eye inflammations. A poultice of eyebright is applied for conjunctivitis, and an infusion as a nasal douche for coughs, colds, sinus infections and allergic rhinitis. John Pechey, writing in 1694, alluded to its use in 'Sallets', and as external medicine for 'when the eye is much bruis'd', or as a wound herb for other parts of the body.

> *Culpeper thought it strengthened the brain and improved memory, even suggesting it as a remedy for vertigo*

Eyebright tea was also recommended for internal use. Culpeper thought it strengthened the brain and improved memory, even suggesting it as a remedy for vertigo. Some herbalists claimed it bestowed second sight and psychic powers, or at the very least insight. The *Countrie Farme* of 1616 advises to 'drinke everie morning a small draught of Eyebright wine', and in the time of Queen Elizabeth I eyebright ale was a popular drink.

In French, eyebright is a spectacles-breaker, *casse-lunette* (so are cornflowers), and local names include fairy flax or bird's eye. *Euphrasia* comes from the Greek meaning 'to cheer', since this little flower would fill the eye-patient with joy.

108

FLEABANE

Pulicaria dysenterica

Fleabane, bane of the flea: hence *Pulicaria*, after the Latin for flea, since the soapy smell of the plant deters fleas and gnats. A strewing herb in medieval times, the dried leaves were also burned on the hearth to rid the house of pests, and used to ward off insects including midges. Dioscorides was the first to note this property in the first century AD, and in the seventeenth Nicholas Culpeper remarked 'the smell is supposed delightful to insects and the juice destructive to them, for they never leave it till the season of their deaths'. Modern analysis shows that the plant contains thymol, which kills houseflies. It was also an ingredient of incense.

The specific *dysenterica* speaks for itself: thus fleabane took a necessary place in the country medicine chest. It also had a reputation as a vulnerary in Arab folklore, where fleabane is known as Job's tears after a legend that he used the bruised leaves of fleabane to relieve the sores he laments of in the Book of Job. Local names include harvest flower (fleabane flowers around harvest time), and pig daisy. It is indeed a member of the daisy family, with sunburst yellow flowers, which the Romans used in wreaths (maybe for its insect-repellent properties as much as its beauty), although Culpeper had low regard for its looks: 'an ill-looking weed, small, very poor and of a dirty yellow'. How unfair. It is a lovely, cheerful, late-flowering wild flower, which attracts several *Lepidoptera* including the powdered Quaker and the small marbled moths.

> *In medieval times, the dried leaves were also burned on the hearth to rid the house of pests*

BLUE FLEABANE
Erigeron acer

SMALL FLEABANE
Pulicaria vulgaris

CANADIAN FLEABANE
Conyza canadensis

IRISH FLEABANE
Inula salicina

FORGET-ME-NOT

Myositis species

That blue and bright-eyes flowerlet of the brook,
Hope's gentle gem, the sweet Forget-me-not.
Coleridge, 'The Keepsake', 1802

Samuel Taylor Coleridge's poem is a melancholy tale of how the forget-me-not got its name. A knight and his lady were strolling along the banks of the Danube on the eve of their wedding when they saw a mist of sky-blue flowers growing on an island in the river. The bride-to-be admired their delicacy, whereupon her lover plunged into the water to gather them for her. He reached the flowers safely, but on his return the current was too strong for him in his heavy armour. As he was swept to his death, he flung the fatal flowers on to the bank crying, 'Forget me not!'

Or, while God was walking through the Garden of Eden after the Creation, He noticed a small blue flower and asked it its name. The flower, overcome by shyness, whispered, 'I'm afraid I've forgotten, Lord.' God answered, 'Forget me not, and I will not forget thee.' Alternatively, God had finished naming all the plants in Eden when a tiny unnamed one cried out, 'Forget me not, O Lord.' God replied, 'That shall be your name.' Or, when Adam missed out the forget-me-not while naming the plants in Paradise, one piped up to ask what she should be called. Adam replied, 'You shall be my forget-me-not.' According to yet another version, as he was naming the flowers of Paradise, he warned them not to forget their names. One little flower took no notice, and promptly forgot its name. Ashamed of its forgetfulness, it asked Adam what he had called it. 'Forget-me-not!' came the reply. And a New Testament legend has the baby Jesus sitting on Mary's lap wishing there were some way to make everyone able to see the blue of her eyes. Take your pick.

Blacksmiths kept a bunch of forget-me-nots in the forge to protect horses from injury

Henry IV, in exile as Duke of Bolingbroke, adopted the forget-me-not as his personal emblem. When he returned to England to take the throne, he retained it as proof of the loyalty of his supporters. The forget-me-not became a symbol of fidelity because it keeps coming back: flower of lovers, of true love and constancy. Lovers would exchange posies of forget-me-nots on parting, believing that whoever wore them would never be forgotten. In France forget-me-nots, known as *ne m'oubliez* pas and *aimez-moi*, were in the height of fashion as a pot plant at the beginning of the nineteenth century, and if you planted them on the grave of the one you loved, the flowers would never die as long as you lived.

Country lore considers it lucky to give forget-me-nots to travellers setting out on 29 February, and advises lovers to exchange forget-me-nots at leap year. Blacksmiths kept a bunch of forget-me-nots in the forge to protect horses from injury, and if steel was tempered with forget-me-not juice, it was able to cut stone. The tufted forget-me-not (*M. laxa*) was made into a syrup as a cough remedy and to cure lung complaints, and in Siberia forget-me-nots were used to cure symptoms of venereal disease.

It's said that clouds of forget-me-nots sprang up on the battlefields after the battle of Waterloo in 1815, and they came to symbolise remembrance of the dead. In 1926, Freemasons adopted the forget-me-not as an emblem for remembering the poor and dispossessed. As the Nazis occupied Europe in the early 1940s, the flower became a means of recognition in place of the Freemason Square and Compass logo, to avoid members being singled out and persecuted by them. To this day the forget-me-not is used to memorialise members victimised by the Nazi regime, or worn to remember those who have died but are not forgotten. The five petals of the forget-me-not with its yellow eye are used as the logo of the Alzheimer's Society.

> *It's said that clouds of forget-me-nots sprang up on the battlefields after the battle of Waterloo*

One of fifty species in the genus *Boraginaceae*, forget-me-nots range from white to pink and from azure to a beautiful pale sky-blue, with a yellow-orange centre. They vary in size according to habitat, flowering from April to July in open woods and grassland, roadsides, gardens and waste ground – as Gerard describes – 'upon most drie and barren ditchbanks'. They also thrive in moist places, and where the ground is particularly wet they may remain in flower until September. Annuals, they self-seed freely, providing food for seed-eating birds. The larvae of several species of *Lepidoptera* feed on their leaves, including the setaceous Hebrew character moth.

Henry David Thoreau considered the forget-me-not 'the more beautiful for being small and unpretending: even flowers must be modest'. The poet Edmund Spenser knew it as starlight, but its most widely used name until the sixteenth century was scorpion grass, after Dioscorides who described its coiled racemes as resembling the tail of a scorpion (this meant by association, of course, that the plant could cure the bites of scorpions, snakes and the ubiquitous 'madde dogs').

Myosotis comes from two Greek words meaning 'mouse' and 'ear', after the shape and softness of the hairy leaf, so forget-me-nots acquired, in the sixteenth century, a common name of mousear. The flower became commonly known as forget-me-not only in the nineteenth century, after Coleridge's dirge became popular. Other names include birds eye, love-me and robin's eye. Of the various varieties' specific names, *arvensis* is 'of the meadows', *sylvatica* 'of the woods', *alpestris* for 'alpine', *ramosissima*, 'early', *laxa*, 'tufted', and *scorpioides* or scorpion grass for water forget-me-not.

WOOD
FORGET-ME-NOT
Myosotis sylvatica

CHANGING
FORGET-ME-NOT
Myosotis discolor

FOXGLOVE

Digitalis purpurea

The foxglove is the fairies' flower, gloves for fairy folk, little folks' glove – or even gloves for foxes, given them to wear by wicked fairies so they can stalk chicken roosts invisibly, or magically elude fox snares, or silently sneak up on their prey, or steal away from their chief predator, mankind. If fairies themselves put the gloves on, there is no magic they cannot do, and although it's dangerous for us to pick foxgloves, being a fairy plant, if we do, we have a defence against their spells.

The resemblance of foxglove flowers to the fingers of a glove, and its habit of growing on disturbed ground near the earths of foxes, contribute to the provenance of its name. The Bavarian physician

Leonhard Fuchs first named it *Digitalis* in 1542, *digitale* meaning 'finger of a glove', or finger-stall, as in the German *Fingerhut*, 'thimble'. In 1568, William Turner describes how it was given its Latin name because of the shape of the flowers: 'There is an herbe groweth very much in Englande, and specially in Norfolke, about ye cony holes in sandy ground, and in diuers woodes, which is called in English "Foxe-gloue", and in Dutch Fingerkraut. It is named of some in Latin "Digitalis", that is to say Thimble-wurt. It hath a long stalke, and in the toppe manye floures hanging doune like belles or thumbles.'

Further back in time, the Anglo-Saxon name was foxes' glew, meaning foxes' music, because to them the corolla was shaped like an ancient musical instrument, a ring of bells hung on an arched support: nature's floral wind chime. Foxgloves acquired numerous local names including granny's gloves, gloves of Our Lady (in France it is *doigts de vierge*, and *dé de Notre Dame*), Our Lady's thimble and goblins' thimble. In Ireland it's fairy cap, since the fairies there wear the flowers as either headgear or gloves, and fairies of the moon were decked in petticoats of foxgloves. In Scotland they are dead men's bells: if you hear them ringing you are not long for this world. Other names include bloody finger, *gant de Venus*, bloody man's fingers, floppydock, beecatchers, bee-hives, Coventry bells, dead men's bellows, dog's fingers and flops. Curiously, this striking plant is not mentioned by Shakespeare or any of the major English poets.

If fairies themselves put the gloves on, there is no magic they cannot do

Varying in colour from magenta through shades of pink to white, the interior of the tubular corolla is mottled with crimson spots on a whitish background. John Ruskin was intrigued: 'the spot of the foxglove is especially strange, because it draws the colour out of the tissue all around it, as if it had been stung, and as if the central colour was really an inflamed spot, with paleness around.' A biennial (occasionally perennial) herbaceous plant, the foxglove is common throughout Britain, flowering from June to September, in partial sunlight to deep shade, in a range of habitats from open woodland and clearings, moorland and heath margins, sea-cliffs, to rocky mountain slopes and

It's unlucky to carry foxgloves on board ship

hedgerows. Its flowers are pollinated by bumblebees, and six species of moths feed on the leaves, including those of the lesser yellow underwing, the frosted orange and the foxglove pug. It is the food plant of the heath fritillary butterfly.

When their tall stalks bend in the wind, it's believed that foxgloves are acknowledging a passing supernatural presence. Elves are said to hide in the bells of the flowers, which give mysterious and magical powers to anyone who holds them (some even fancied the spots as elves' fingerprints). The Druids revered the foxglove and used it in midsummer rituals, it being in full flower around that time. In flower language, foxgloves represent pride before a fall, and it's unlucky to carry foxgloves on board ship. Never bring them into the house, because devils and witches will come in with them (allegedly foxgloves were an ingredient of an ointment which, rubbed on witches' legs, enabled them to fly: its other ingredients were baby fat, the hallucinatory belladonna and hemlock, which induces unconsciousness). Conversely, foxgloves growing in your garden are a protective plant, because good fairies will colonise them, and keep evil away.

The foxglove is one of the most poisonous plants in our flora, to humans, livestock and poultry as well as dogs and cats. 'The operation of this herb, internally taken, is often violent, even in small doses: it is best therefore not to meddle with it, lest the cure should end in the churchyard', comments one of the early herbalists. Leonhard Fuchs, he who gave it its Latin name, considered it a drastic medicine. Yet it is the source of the most potent and widely used substances in the treatment of heart disease. Foxgloves contain cardiac glycosides that strengthen and regulate heartbeat, while stimulating urine production, which keeps blood pressure down. The critical compound that acts so powerfully on the heart muscle, digitalin, is extracted from the dried and powdered leaves. It was discovered by William Wittering in Shropshire in 1785, who describes in his *An Account of the Foxglove and Some of its Medical Uses* how digoxin slows down the movement of the heart. He went on to use it in the treatment of dropsy (accumulation of fluid in parts of the body), and digitalin is still used in generalised oedema. Wittering had discovered a potent drug that has saved many lives, and he has a foxglove carved on his tomb in Edgbaston Old Church.

Foxglove leaves can be applied externally as a compress or poultice for the treatment of wounds. You can add an infusion from the leaves to make a vase of cut flowers last longer (but don't drink it, it's poisonous). And it's a good companion plant: when potatoes and root vegetables, tomatoes and apples are grown near foxgloves, they store better. The wackiest of recommendations comes from Nicholas Culpeper: 'I am confident that an ointment of it is one of the best remedies for a scabby head that is.'

Foxgloves were an ingredient of an ointment which, rubbed on witches' legs, enabled them to fly

LARGE YELLOW FOXGLOVE
Digitalis grandiflora

FUMITORY

Fumaria officinalis

Fumitory is earth smoke, *fume-terre*, and when you pull the roots from the ground it actually smells smoky, the smell resembling nitric acid. North Americans still call it fume root, the name going back to an old belief that the plant was created out of mist rising from the ground – and it's true that, from a distance, a bed of fumitory with its pale blueish-green leaves looks like dispersing smoke. Pliny called it *Fumaria*, saying that the plant got its name from causing the eyes to water, as smoke does when it gets in your eyes. A familiar arable weed, fumitory is nectar-rich but – perhaps because of its odour – insects seem to avoid it (although cattle and sheep will graze on it), so the flowers self-pollinate. The increasingly rare turtle dove feeds on its shoots and seeds. Its scent has led to its use in incense mixtures and for exorcisms.

Dioscorides reported that the juice of fumitory dropped into the eyes clears the sight, also describing how when this juice is dissolved in gum arabic and applied to the skin around plucked eyebrows, it will prevent them growing again. A decoction of fumitory was said to be effective for removing cradle-cap in newborn infants. According to the thirteenth-century Franciscan monk Bartolomeus Anglicus, the roots have a 'horrible savour' but can be made into a potion for dispelling melancholy. Later herbalists found it effective in curing intestinal diseases and, over time, from Disocorides to Chaucer and as far east as Japan, fumitory acquired a reputation as a purifier of the blood. Or the soul: 'if you wish to be pure and holy/wash your face with fumitory' – originally a recipe for clearing freckles this, according to a Victorian practitioner, 'ought chiefly to be employed by those who have previously removed those moral blemishes which deform the mind, or degrade the dignity of a reasonable and an immortal being.'

> *If you wish to be pure and holy/ wash your face with fumitory*

The medicinal effects of fumitory are tonic, diaphoretic (inducing perspiration), diuretic and laxative. Analysis shows it to contain fumaric acid, used nowadays as a food additive (the non-toxic acidity regulator listed as E297). It is added to beverages and baking powders for which requirements are placed on purity.

For good luck, scatter fumitory around the house, or rub it into your shoes. In Germany it is the thunderer's plant, and protects against evil. Local names include babe in the cradle, God's fingers and thumbs, lady's lockets, and lady's shoe. The specific *officinalis* denotes that the plant merited a place in the country medicine chest.

GARLIC MUSTARD

Alliaria petiolata

Known to many as hedge garlic or Jack-by-the-hedge – 'Jack' being a term of friendly familiarity – garlic mustard is among the first spring wild flowers to show in banks and hedgerows, standing like a sentinel with soft broad leaves and heads of bright white flowers. Dozens of insects feed on it, as do the larvae of the garden carpet moth. speckled woods, orange tips, and the green-veined and small white butterflies nectar on it. A member of the mustard family, and called poor man's mustard, it was also known as sauce alone because its crushed leaves, smelling of garlic, were added to springtime sauces and salads. In 1657 William Coles remarked that it is 'eaten by many country people as sauce to their salt fish, and helpeth well to digest the crudities and other crude humours that are engendered by the eating thereof.'

According to an early herbalist, 'the seed bruised and boiled in wine is a good remedy for the wind, colic or the stone, if drunk warm.' The plant is mildly antiseptic, and a poultice was applied

> *Garlic mustard is a remedy for asthma, and sniffed into the nostrils will revive an hysteric*

as dressings to open sores and ulcers. Having diuretic properties, the leaves were used in country medicine for dropsy, and to induce sweating. A syrup of garlic mustard is a remedy for asthma, and sniffed into the nostrils will revive an hysteric.

123

GOLDENROD

Solidago virgaurea

Growing up to 2ft (60cm) tall, goldenrod acquired a local name of Farewell Summer from its late flowering. From July to September its eye-catching yellow flowers can be found on mountainsides, copses and banks, in woods and hedgerows and dry meadows, although it is rarely found growing wild in East Anglia and the Midlands (cultivars have proved popular garden plants, however).

Goldenrod's botanical name comes from the Latin *consolida* meaning 'to make whole' or heal. Goldenrod's principal medicinal use was as a vulnerary in days when stab wounds were common, and Gerard writes that it 'is extolled above all other herbes for the stopping of bloud in bleeding wounds'. A poultice expedited tissue-healing, and an infusion cleared up infected areas, internal and external. Its anti-fungal saponins were useful in treating candida and oral thrush. It made a mouthwash for thrush, catarrh and throat infections, and was said to ease asthma, arthritis and rheumatism. Goldenrod affects the action of the kidneys and liver, and being a powerful diuretic was used from the thirteenth century onwards to treat urinary tract infections as well as kidney stones, dropsy, cystitis and nephritis.

In the sixteenth century, goldenrod as medicine became so popular that large amounts of the dried plant were imported at half a crown an ounce. But it lost its commercial value when, as Gerard describes, the plant was discovered growing wild in Hampstead, 'even as it were at our townes end'. One of its local names, Aaron's rod, refers to a passage in Numbers (xvii, 8) where the Lord instructs Moses to take twelve rods and write the name of Aaron on one of them: 'And it came to pass, that on the morrow Moses went into the tabernacle of witness; and behold, the rod of Aaron for the house of Levi was budded, and brought forth buds, and bloomed blossoms ...' Goldenrod was used as a divining rod, not only for springs, but also for hidden treasure and hoards of gold and silver. Amerindians used the seeds in food, they chewed the leaves to relieve sore throats and the roots to relieve toothache. In some places the plant signifies good luck. If it grows close to your main door it will bring good fortune to everyone in the household. A golden-yellow dye can be made from the flowers, as well as a herbal tea, and the plant was once used to produce a poor-quality rubber. Goldenrod is the state flower of Kentucky, Nebraska and South Carolina.

Goldenrod's pollen is sometimes blamed for causing hayfever, but is too heavy to be windblown and the offending pollen is more likely to be of ragwort (goldenrod is mainly insect-pollinated). Nectar from its flowers attract bees, hoverflies, wasps and about 40 species of moth including the increasingly rare white spotted sable moth, and four of the plume moths. Goldenrod leaves are a food source for larvae of the bordered pearl, the wormwood pug and the peppered moths.

Local names include *verge d'or*, wound weed and golden wings.

GOOSEGRASS

Galium aparine

Goosegrass is what it says on the tin, food for geese and goslings: according to a fifteenth-century manuscript in the British Museum it was chopped up and put into their feed, and given to poultry too: 'He wol make gees and hennes fatte if this herbe be brok smal among hure mete.' It was also believed to cure them of disease. *Aparine* comes from *apo*, a Latin verb meaning 'to fasten', after the burrs, giving goosegrass the name loveman because of its clinging habit. Other local names include cleavers, gosling grass, sticky Billy, beggar lice, clinging sweethearts and Robin-run-the-hedge. According to Dioscorides, the hairy, sticky leaves were used by shepherdesses to strain hairs out of milk, and 15 centuries later William Turner noted how 'shepherds use cleavers in stede of a strayner to pull out here [hair] of the mylke'. Clearly it had its place in the dairy: goosegrass's generic name *Galium* comes from the Greek for milk, *gala*, in common with lady's bedstraw (*G. verum*), since both plants curdle milk. The roots are red, and yield a red dye. Seven moths are known to visit goosegrass, among them the yellow shell and the barred straw.

Goosegrass is what it says on the tin, food for geese and goslings

A vigorous, bright green annual and the despair of gardeners, goosegrass is unusual in that most wild climbers are perennial. However, it seeds so prolifically that it's hard to eradicate – but useful to some: a fascinating snippet of cultural history is that lacemakers would stick these seeds on to their pins to give them a larger head. The plant is rich in silica, calcium and sodium, and infusions are beneficial for the hair and teeth. In country medicine it was used for sores and skin complaints like acne and eczema, for scurvy (it's also known as scurvy grass), for ulcers and, being a relative of quinine, for sore throats, jaundice, scarlet fever and measles. It's a general all-round spring tonic, and according to Mrs Grieve in *A Modern Herbal*, an infusion of goosegrass 'has a most soothing effect in cases of insomnia, and induces quiet, restful sleep'.

Diet for the goose, perhaps, not so appetising to man, although the young shoots can be made into soup. However, the roasted seeds have been used as a coffee substitute (botanically it's a relative), and Gerard records goosegrass as an ingredient of a sixteenth-century slimming diet (aversion therapy?): 'Women do usually make potage of Cleavers with a little mutton and oatmeale, to cause lankenesse, and to keep them from fatness.'

Gerard records goosegrass as an ingredient of a sixteenth-century slimming diet (aversion therapy?)

GREATER CELANDINE

Chelidonium majus

Greater celandine is a member of the poppy family and, although poisonous, was regarded in folk medicine as a cure-all – indeed the ancients regarded it as a gift from God. Common throughout the British Isles, it flowers in hedgerows, at the feet of stone walls, in waste places and gardens from April to October. It's a tall weed with soft, greyish-green lobed leaves, and delicate branched stems bearing clusters of custard-yellow flowers. The botanical name *Chelidonium* derives from the Greek *chelidon*, 'a swallow', and medieval herbalists maintained that swallows picked 'swallow-wort' to apply juice from the stems to the eyes of their young: 'with this herbe the dams restore sight to their young ones when their eyes be put out', says John Gerard in his *Herbal* of 1597.

Used for thousands of years to improve eyesight, and cultivated since Anglo-Saxon times as a medicinal herb, the orangey-yellow latex from its stems was popular among village simplers as a remedy, mixed with milk, for human eye disorders: 'the juice is good to sharpen the sight, for it cleanseth and consumeth awaie slimie things that cleave about the ball of the eye'. They called it yellow spit, or kenning wort, a kenning being a cloudy spot on the eyeball. Greater celandine was used in Chinese medicine, too, for bronchitis, whooping cough and asthma. Once lovingly cultivated in the garden and now rejected as a weed, its flowers are carved on the thirteenth-century shrine of St Frideswide in Oxford's Christ Church cathedral. A benefactress of the blind, the saint summoned up a holy well in the village of Binsey near Oxford, using its waters to heal eye and stomach problems.

Herbalists have found that greater celandine does in fact act as an antispasmodic on the bladder and gallbladder, and they prescribe it to relieve inflammation of the bile duct. According to the Doctrine of Signatures, it's an infallible remedy for jaundice, in addition to which the root turns yellow when put into white wine. Less credibly, wear this witches' flower near the skin to escape from your enemies, or to lift the spirits, dispel melancholy and cure depression.

The fresh juice of greater celandine can be applied to verrucas, ringworm and warts, as reflected in local names kill-wart and wartwort – or, as John Clare called it, wartweed: 'the yellow juice emitted when the stalk is broken is applyd to warts as a certain cure & I myself have known it suceed often––my mother has a poetical superstition about them she calls ... them Dane weed as they grow plentifully in a field at her native place were it is said the danes and redshanks fought a desperate battle & on that day which it is said to be Whit sunday she assures me for certain tho she never tryd it herself that they emit a red juice instead of a yellow I have never had the curosity to travel so far to contradict her'.

GREATER STITCHWORT

Stellaria holostea

A plant to cure a stitch in the side: to the Anglo-Saxons and Celts such a pain was likely to be caused by elf-shot, delivered by defending elves to whom stitchwort, also known as pixie flower, belongs. Anyone picking this flower would be led astray by the pixies, who hide in it. Or is it a flower protected by the Devil, Jack-a-lantern of the goblin and plant of the snakes? Known in some parts as Devil's shirt-buttons and Devil's plaything, conversely it's also a flower to banish evil, belonging to the Virgin Mary (in common with many white flowers) and associated with Whitsuntide. Its association with Mary led to a local French name *collerette de la Vierge*, 'Our Lady's little collar'. It's pretty enough to be a poor man's buttonhole, too, and has a local name of daddy's shirt-buttons.

The milk-white, star-shaped flowers of this straggly perennial have also been called star of Bethlehem. The pure white petals, split halfway down into long lobes, spangle grassy banks under hedgerows, and glow along the woodland rides and roadsides where stitchwort flourishes in late spring. In *The Open Air*, published in 1885, Richard Jefferies wrote, 'There shone on the banks white stars among the grass, petals delicately white in a whorl of rays – light that had started radiating from a centre and become fixed – shining among the flowerless green ... Give me that old road, the same flowers – they were only stitchwort ...'

To some, stitchwort is a thunder-flower, causing thunder and lightning if you pick it. Others know it as adders' meat because stitchwort grows in grassy habitats where snakes live: in Cornwall children were taught not to pick it in case adders bit them, others believed that vipers lurked in stitchwort, and if you were lucky enough not to get a snake bite you risked being struck by lightning. A shade-loving plant, the flower wilts quickly when picked and has weak brittle stems which break easily, hence a country name of snapdragon.

Stitchwort is the food plant of *Coleophora lithargyrinella* and several other species of moth, as well as attracting a number of butterflies, beetles, bees and hoverflies. Its specific name *holostea* comes from two Greek words meaning 'whole' and 'bone', from its accredited use in healing broken bones. Medicinally, it was also thought that its use would ensure the production of male children.

Stitchwort's generic name *stellaria* comes from the Latin *stella*, 'star', after its starry flowers that radiate light along springtime hedgerows. Numerous local names include bachelor's buttons, eyebright, shirt buttons, smocks, milkmaids, star flower and starwort. Names like Jack-in-the-box, pop Jack, pop gun and poppers come from its habit of firing off its seeds when they are ripe, providing easy pickings for small seed-eating birds especially linnets, sparrows and finches.

GROUND IVY

Glechoma hederacea

Early in spring this pretty wild flower creeps rampantly, like ivy, along hedgerows and in copses, and is often seen in oak woods. It's so common that it's easy to ignore, but is a little gem with small heart-shaped leaves and blue-purple flowers growing up the stem, to which the red twin-spot, the dark-barred twin-spot and the gold spangle moths are attracted. Ground ivy was used to flavour ale before hops were introduced to England, since it was also found to improve its keeping qualities, as witnessed by local names of alehoof and tunhoof: 'It not only helps to fine it but corrects its Fogginess and enriches it with Salutary Qualities,' writes an early commentator. The juice of the leaves, tunned up in ale, was thought to cure jaundice, and steeping a handful of leaves in boiling water makes a tea called gill tea, a spring tonic to purify the blood and stimulate the appetite. A local name of gill-over-the-ground comes from the French *guiller*, 'to ferment ale'. Ground ivy is related to mint and catmint, sage and lavender, and has a high vitamin C content. It's edible, and one traditional English recipe describes pork with ground ivy leaves in the stuffing.

In the second century AD Galen was aware of the use of ground ivy for treating inflamed eyes, and in the time of Queen Elizabeth I, herb women walked up and down Cheapside in London with baskets of simples, which included ground ivy for making a lotion to soothe tired or sore eyes, a remedy still offered by herbalists for itchiness caused by hayfever and other allergies. Gerard wrote that equal quantities of ground ivy, celandine and daisies stamped and strained with a little sugar and rose water, dropped with a feather into the eyes, 'taketh away all manner of inflammation, spots, webs, itchs, smarting'. Ground ivy was used in lung complaints such as asthma, and at one time was the medicine of hope for consumptives. An infusion of the leaves was applied to bruises and this tea was diuretic and drunk, sweetened with honey, to cure a cough and as a remedy for kidney complaints. Now known for its gentle tonic, diuretic and anti-catarrhal action on the mucous membranes of ear, nose and throat, it is prescribed

Before hops were introduced into England in the sixteenth century, ground ivy was widely used to clarify and flavour ale

for children's catarrh, glue ear, sinusitis and general throat and chest problems. It is also prescribed in herbal medicine for gastritis and acid indigestion. This modest plant, also called creeping Jenny, hedge maids, cat's food, even extends to cheering away melancholy and, stretching credibility, curing lunacy.

GROUNDSEL

Senecio vulgaris

According to its Anglo-Saxon name, groundsel is a ground-swallower, so greedy for land that in the north of England it's known as grundy-swallow, a ground-devourer. But it's not all bad: groundsel's redeeming feature is that it provides a valuable source of iron to the soil in which it grows. It provides sustenance for seven moths including the sword-grass, the small mottled willow and the wood tiger. Traditionally it was best known for feeding canaries and other cage birds, as well as being fed to pigs and goats, rabbits and poultry. Its generic name means 'old man': in the words of William Turner 'the floure of this herbe hath white hayre, and when the wynde bloweth it awaie then it appeareath like a Bald-headed man, therefore it is called "Senecio".' In some parts it has the delightful local name of goblin's shaving brush.

Large doses of groundsel are toxic, although a weak tea made from groundsel is purgative, but medicinally the plant is taken only in small amounts since it can damage the liver. In the past, groundsel ointment was applied to sores and wounds, and a poultice laid on ulcers and tumours. Pouring boiling water over fresh groundsel softens the water and makes a soothing lotion for chapped hands and roughened skin. It also cures toothache, according to Pliny, as well as relieving liver complaints and dysmenorrhoea – and 'bleared or dropping eyes', according to Lyte in 1578. Culpeper recommended it for 'inflammation or watering of the Eyes by reason of the Defluxion of Rheum into them'. Gerard comes up with 'it helpeth the King's Evil and the leaves stamped and strayend into mylke and drunk helpeth the red gums and frets in children'.

Highland women used to wear a piece of groundsel root to avert the Evil Eye

Highland women used to wear a piece of groundsel root to avert the Evil Eye, and to fend off ague. Groundsel was reputed to have combined with lady's bedstraw, thyme and woodruff for the Virgin Mary's childbed.

STICKY GROUNDSEL
Senecio viscosus

HAREBELL
Campanula rotundifolia

T he exquisite harebell, palest violet-blue on fragile stalk, bears nodding bell-shaped flowers, ethereal fairy blossoms to be worn only by faithful lovers:

> *The harebell, for her stainless azure hue,*
> *Claims to be worn of none but who are true.*

But the harebell is also Devils' bell and old man's bell, thought to bring bad luck: woe betide you if you pick it, because it is the Devil himself in disguise. Harebell is also a flower of witches, used by witches as thimbles while making the flying ointments that enable them to see fairies, goblins and earth spirits. Or even to transform themselves into hares, renowned in country lore as a witch's animal. Maybe the harebell grows in the haunts of hares where they make their ground nests: after all, if the fox has his gloves, why should the hare not have his bells?

Confusingly, the Scots call harebell bluebell, and although the wiry stems bear thin linear leaves, the specific name *rotundifolia* describes the rounded basal leaves. This flower is the 'the azured hare-bell' of Shakespeare's *Cymbeline*, and is dedicated to St Dominic. Growing on chalk grassland and heath, cliff faces and dunes, harebells flowers from late spring through to September or even later, pollinated by bees or self-pollinated, and attracting the northern rustic moth.

> *Woe betide you if you pick it, because it is the Devil himself in disguise*

HAWKWEEDS
AND HAWKBITS

Hieracium species

S wathes of small, relatively nondescript yellow flowers appearing in late summer on grassy verges, rough pasture and waste ground, may belong to any number of species: nipplewort, sow-thistle, cat's tongue, ragwort, the dandelion family, the hawk-bits and hawks-beards – and the hawkweeds. Even botanists describe these groups as extremely complicated and difficult to identify (there are 245 species of hawkweed in Britain alone). To the uninitiated they look much the same, and identification is often only through the leaves. Although some of the flowers are lemon-yellow, others are buttercup-gold, but even this difference is marginal.

Hieracium is the Greek for a hawk. The hawk was a bird held in veneration and regarded as sacred, and in ancient Greece hawkweed was a holy plant. Pliny says it got its name 'because hawks tear it apart and wet their eyes with the juice, so dispelling dimness of sight, when it comes on them'. It was commonly believed by falconers, presumably on the evidence, that hawks feed on hawkweed to sharpen their phenomenal eyesight (buzzards have distance vision six to eight times better than humans, and hovering kestrels spot prey up to 70ft below). According to folklore, hawks squeezed the juice out of the plant and rubbed it on their eyeballs, and mother hawks would teach their young to do this.

> *It was commonly believed by falconers, presumably on the evidence, that hawks feed on hawkweed to sharpen their phenomenal eyesight*

Hawkweeds produce seed asexually, and the buttercup-yellow flowers attract bees and flies and the large yellow underwing moth. Mouse-ear hawkweed (*H. pilosella*), a clear lemon-yellow flower often flushed with red, was used in herbal remedies for whooping cough and lung complaints, as well as haemorrhoids. The Victorian botanist Anne Pratt wrote 'the juice thereof taken in wine, or the decoction drank, helpeth the jaundice, although of long continuance, if drank night and morning'. Parkinson claimed 'if Mouseare be given to any hors it will cause that he shall not be hurt by the smith that shooeth him'.

Orange hawkweed (*H. aurantiacum*) is known as grim the collier in mining districts, after its smut-coloured calyx reminiscent of coal-dust. Parkinson describes how 'it groweth in the shadowie woods of France, by Lyons and Mompelier. The French use it for defects of the lunges, but with what good success I know not'. According to folk medicine, it has antibiotic action and makes an effective gargle.

Autumn hawkbit (*Leontodon autumnalis* – lion's tooth, after the jagged leaves), with its deep yellow flowers appearing during August and September, has a honey-like scent. Rough hawkbit (*L. hispidus*), appearing during August and September, used to be recommended for kidney complaints and dropsy, and is a powerful diuretic. Cat's ear (*Hypochaeris radicata*), attracting many insects and particularly bees from June onwards, gets its botanical name from two Greek words meaning 'under' and 'pig', since pigs loved to forage for the roots. It's called cat's ear after the scale-like bracts that spiral up the flower stems, by which the plant can be easily identified.

Ragwort (*Senecio jacobaea*) also appears in late summer, in similar habitats. Its generic name means old man, after the fluffy white seedheads, and is a 'rag' plant because of the ragged-looking leaves. Its specific name is after St James, patron and protector of horses, because it was mistakenly believed that an infusion of ragwort in small doses was a cure for the staggers, an infection which affects the equine brain and spinal cord. But actually ragwort is poisonous to all livestock: the leaves contain toxic alkaloids that linger after the plant is cut, and although horses and cattle usually avoid eating it because of its bitter taste, the plant can be fatal if it finds its way into hay. The active ingredient has no known antidote, and destroys the liver over a period of months. Ragwort is now classified as an 'injurious weed' with an accompanying code of practice, which does not however impose legal responsibility on a landowner to control it.

In folk medicine, ragwort was used to cure eye inflammations, cancerous sores and painful joints. In Ancient Greece and Rome it was called Satyrion, and supposed to be aphrodisiac. The leaves yield a green dye, the flowers a yellow. Ragwort is the food plant of the endearing bronze-coloured ragwort flea beetle, introduced in some areas to combat the spread of the plant. Ragwort provides a food source for many other insects including hoverflies, solitary bees, moths and butterflies including the small copper, as well as to nineteen moths including the ruby tiger, the cinnabar and the beautiful golden.

The Scots call ragwort stinking Billy because of the unpleasant smell of the leaves when bruised, the Billy in question being son of King George II, William Duke of Cumberland, who won the battle of Culloden in 1746 – not the most flattering of memorials. Other common names for ragwort include benweed, tansy ragwort, St James wort, ragweed, stinking nanny or ninny-willy, staggerwort, dog standard, cankerwort, stammerwort, mare's fart and cushag.

MOUSE-EAR HAWKWEED
Hieracium pilosella

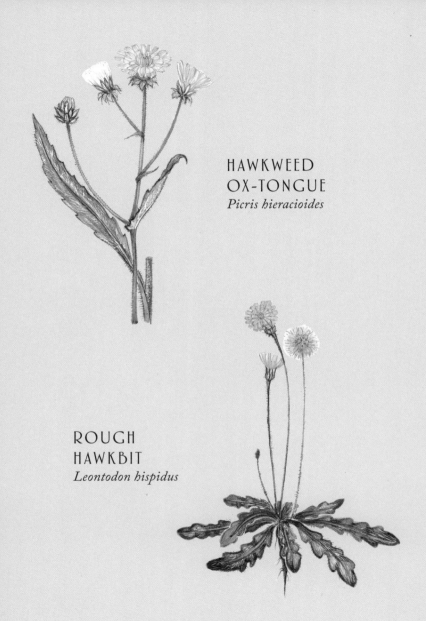

HAWKWEED
OX-TONGUE
Picris hieracioides

ROUGH
HAWKBIT
Leontodon hispidus

LEAFY
HAWKWEED
Hieracium umbellatum

AUTUMN
HAWKBIT
Leontodon autumnalis

143

HERB ROBERT

Geranium robertianum

Herb Robert, like the robin, is found everywhere near human habitation as well as in wild places and hedgebanks. It loves to scramble up old walls and ruins, over waste ground and rubble, around gardens and across roofs of solitary farmhouses, like that haunter of the hearth our house-goblin, the mischievous sprite Robin Goodfellow, to whom we must offer cream and courtesy if he is to desist from mischief. Herb Robert, a cranesbill, flowers from early in the year until late in the autumn with deep pink flowers veined with red, long-beaked fruits and hairy stems that turn red in bright light, and ferny, slightly hairy leaves. It was so loved and admired in the Middle Ages that it was cultivated in flower gardens much as our geraniums are today. *Geranos* is Greek for 'crane', after the spiky fruits that resemble the bill of the Eurasian crane.

Herb Robert is associated with goblins and magic, and possesses a mixture of good and bad properties: like the robin, it brings good luck if it is treated well, but bad luck if it isn't (in the robin's case when its nest is destroyed or, especially, if it's killed). In Cumberland, it's unlucky to pick Herb Robert, which has a local name of death-come-quickly. Because of its unpleasant smell, it is an effective insect-repellent, hence local names of stinking Bob and stink flowers, because, according to Gerard, 'it hath a most lothsome stinking smell'. It's also known as red Robin, bloodwort, granny's needle, hedge lovers, jam tarts, poor Robert, redbreasts and snake flower. Geoffrey Grigson's *Englishman's Flora* lists no fewer than 111 vernacular names.

> *Geoffrey Grigson's An Englishman's Flora lists no fewer than 111 vernacular names*

When the flowers hang downwards it's a sign of impending bad weather. The Victorian botanist Anne Pratt observed, 'when growing in exposed situations, the stems and leaves have a rich crimson colour, and often in autumn, when they linger on a bank, they are almost as beautiful as the flowers themselves'. As Wordsworth commented, 'Poor Robin is yet flowerless, but how gay with his red stalks upon this sunny day'. These red stems gave the *herba roberti* of apothecaries' medieval Latin the appellation of *herba rubra*, and by association the plant was effective, by the Doctrine of Signatures, in staunching the flow of blood. Classified as an official medicinal herb in the Middle Ages, Herb Robert was a wound healer, and still features in folk medicine for stomach and digestive complaints, as well as for kidney and bladder infections. In homeopathy the flowers and leaves, rich in tannins, are prescribed as a remedy for diarrhoea, or applied to slow-healing lesions. Herb Robert was made into a poultice for inflammations, and a compress from the crushed leaves was a remedy for skin eruptions and bruises. It was made into an eyewash, and in

Wales was a cure for gout. An infusion from the leaves was gargled for throat and mouth infections. Culpeper agreed that it could indeed cure all these ailments: 'You may persuade yourself this is true and conceive a good reason for it.'

Herb Robert may have got its name from the eleventh-century St Robert of Molesme who founded Cîteaux Abbey in France, later the seat of the Cistercian Order under St Bernard. It's said that he staunched wounds and healed ulcers with the plant. St Robert's feast day falls on 29 April when Herb Robert is coming into flower, and he was invoked to help cure these conditions. Other sources maintain that the plant was named after Robert, Duke of Normandy, son of William the Conqueror and patron of medical botany, who used Herb Robert to cure the plague —'Ruprecht's-plage', Robert's plague. A celebrated treatise was addressed to Duke Robert in which *Geranium robertianum* is named as an official herb: *The Salerno Book of Health* opens with the timeless advice: 'Use three Physicians still; first Doctor Quiet, Next Doctor Merry-man, and Doctor Diet.'

HOGWEED

Heracleum sphondylium

Growing in hedgerows, woods and grassy places, hogweed can reach the height of a tall man. This handsome umbellifer, with white flowerheads supported on umbrella ribs, delights in names of cow clogweed, humpy-scrumples, humperscrump, madnep and pig's flop. The plant was used as pig and cattle fodder, so in the past it was a not uncommon sight to see country folk carrying bundles of hogweed – also familiar to them as pigweed and cow-parsnip (the name given by William Turner in the sixteenth century, possibly because of the pungent sweetish scent of the flowers, which resembles cowdung) – back to the farmyard. The smell, sometimes also described as pig-like, attracts the pernicious carpet beetle (which you do not want to allow into your house). The tiny florets produce abundant nectar, and you often see them crawling with flies and beetles, especially species with a short proboscis – and they attract 16 varieties of moth. In July, hogweed flowers are the mating ground for the bright orange soldier or July beetle (*Rhagonycha fulva*).

In spite of the off-putting fragrance, the young shoots of hogweed provide food-for-free, a poor man's asparagus, which, lightly steamed and served with butter, is surprisingly tasty. Also edible are the young stems, which can be peeled and served raw in salads. When mature, the deeply furrowed stems are hollow, and popular

Delights in names of Cow Clogweed, Humpy-scrumples, Humperscrump, Madnep and Pig's Flop

with children as pea-shooters, but ensure that you don't confuse the plant with its cousin the giant hogweed (*H. manteganzzianum*), whose purple blotched stem grows up to 3m (10ft) tall: it is highly toxic, and just handling it can cause severe burns and blistering, leaving long-term scars and making the skin sensitive to sunlight for years.

Legend goes that Hercules (or, in Greek, Heracles) discovered the medicinal properties of this robust plant, hence the generic name *Heracleum*. It was used to relieve hypertension and to treat epilepsy, and had sedative, expectorant and tonic properties. The seeds are said to be aphrodisiac, and hogweed retains a place in homeopathic medicine for spinal complaints, epilepsy, headaches and stomach pain. Its specific name *Sphondylium* comes from the Greek for vertebra, from the joints along the stems.

HONEYSUCKLE

Lonicera pericylmenum

Widely quoted in poetry from Chaucer onwards as the flower of love, honeysuckle was an emblem of fidelity, traditionally presented by lovers to each other to demonstrate undying passion. Often planted to enclose a garden bower, the fragrance is said to induce dreams of love. In flower language, honeysuckle stands for generous and devoted affection, representing constancy.

Also called goat's leaf, honeysuckle climbs like a mountain goat beyond the places where man dares to tread, and its other name woodbine comes from its habit of twining itself into the branches of trees. It's also known as hold-me-tight, eglantine, fairy trumpets, evening pride, honeybind and withywind. Samuel Pepys, in uncharacteristically romantic mode, described how its 'ivory bugles blow scent instead of sound', nicknaming it trumpet flower. The name honeysuckle itself derives from the sweet nectar in the corollas, which makes them tempting to children to suck (the bright red berries on the other hand, are mildly poisonous). *L. periclymenum* grows freely in hedgerows and along woodland edges, and William Turner wrote in 1548 of our native climber, 'Woodbyne is commune in every woodde'. John Parkinson reckoned that it shouldn't be brought into the garden, but left in the wild for the enjoyment of the passer-by: 'The honeysuckle that groweth wilde in every hedge, although it be very sweete, yet doe I not bring into my garden, but let it rest in its owne place to serve their senses that travel by it, or have no garden.'

Witches used garlands of honeysuckle in spells to cure sick children and to repel evil spirits on May Day. Scottish herb women used it in simple remedies for children, and their farmers used to place branches of honeysuckle in the cowshed on 2 May, to protect livestock from being bewitched as well as to take care of the milk and butter. If you planted it near the house, it would stop witches entering; if it grew well in the garden you would be protected from evil; and bringing the flowers into the house would bring money with them. Gerard says the 'the floures steeped in oile and set in the sun, are good to annoint the body that is benummed, and growne very cold'. The honeysuckle Bach Flower Remedy is said 'to remove from the mind the regrets and sorrows of the past and to bring the patient back to the present'.

Used as an antispasmodic in herbal medicine, dried honeysuckle flowers can be used for bronchial coughs, asthma and sore throats. Being rich in salicylic acid they have been proved good for rheumatism, headaches and fevers, colds and flu, and the fresh flowers infused in runny honey make an effective remedy for sore throats. The flowers can also be added to teas, vinegars, jams and jellies for their delicate flavour.

There are 180 species worldwide of this hardy, twining climber, and the powerful scent released in the evening attracts flying insects and many *Lepidoptera*. The flowers are pollinated by no fewer than 25 species of moth including hawk-moths, and also long-tongued bees. Birds are attracted to the berries in autumn, and the dense tangles of stems provide nesting sites. In Celtic folklore, honeysuckle is particularly associated with the lapwing. The stems were used for binding and in textile making, the hard wood of the thicker stems made into tobacco pipes.

Farmers used to place branches of honeysuckle in the cowshed on 2 May, to protect livestock from being bewitched

Linnaeus named *Lonicera* after Adam Lonicer, a German botanist who died in 1586. Its specific name *periclymenum* comes from the Greek meaning 'entwine around'.

152

HOP

Humulus lupulus

Although native to Britain, hops were regarded with suspicion until the reign of Henry VIII. Before that, beer was brewed from wild plants such as dandelion, burdock, mugwort, horehound, yarrow and (especially) ground ivy. In the fifteenth century, hops were 'that wicked weed', their addition to beer considered so bitter it was tantamount to adding brimstone, they said. Hops were prohibited under strict penalties, and in 1519 were still recorded as 'that wicked and pernicious weed', but by 1524 commercial quantities were being introduced from Flanders to be cultivated in England. Within a short time hops replaced other plants as the basic ingredient of beer, as they were found to make it last longer (hops have an antibacterial effect, which acts as a preservative). Their bitterness, counteracting the sweetness of malt, and the flavour they impart, became the acquired taste of the day. Fashions change, times change:

> *In the reign of Elizabeth I, an edict was issued to restrain the use of 'this pernicious weed the hop'*

> *Hops and Reformation, bays and beer,*
> *Came to England all in one year.*

There was a reaction in the reign of Elizabeth I, when an edict was issued to restrain the use of 'this pernicious weed the hop', but the ruling failed and hops are with us still, a major crop in Kent and Sussex where they are harvested and dried in oast houses (from the Dutch *eest huis*, drying house, designed to create natural draughts through the cones at the top of the building). Hops continued to flourish in the wild, sometimes as an escape, so nothing has changed much since William Turner wrote in 1548, 'Hoppes do growe by hedges and busshes both set and unset.'

It's said that when hops were planted near Doncaster, the nightingale made its first appearance there. At the end of the hop harvest a Hop Queen was traditionally crowned in the middle of the field to celebrate the accomplished task. In Russia, hops are considered the best of wild plants, and there was an old country custom of presenting a bride with a hop garland to bring joy, abundance and intoxication to her marriage.

Invalids used to be wheeled from convalescent homes to inhale the aroma from nearby fragrant hop fields

Yet in flower language the hop stands for injustice, since its climbing tendrils stifle the plants it entwines, and its prodigious growth uses up nutrients in the soil. Its generic botanical name *Humulus* comes from *humus*, 'earth', as it thrives on rich soils. The Anglo-Saxon *hoppen* means 'to climb' (or maybe just to hop), and an old Latin word *homnel* means a plant with twisting, exploring tendrils 'which gropes and fumbles around'. *Lupulus* is more obscure: first used by Brunfels in the early sixteenth century, he was echoing an ancient expression *lupus salictarius*, wolf of the willows. The hop is like a wolf devouring its prey as branches of the willow are enveloped by the vine's prolific growth. This clinging habit means that hop has love associations too.

The female plant bears beautiful cone-like green flowers from July to September, so fragrant that invalids used to be wheeled from convalescent homes to inhale the aroma from nearby hop fields. The yellowish powder extracted from hop cones, *lupulin*, is sedative, stimulates the appetite and calms nerves (hops are related to cannabis), and animal research shows it to have similar effects. Dried hops are made into hop pillows to help nervous irritation and sleeplessness, and one was presented to King George III who regularly used it. Hop tea is soporific and slightly narcotic, reduces cravings for alcohol, encourages liver function and helps digestion, and is slightly aphrodisiac. Hops featured in the *British Pharmacopoeia* until recently, but are poisonous to dogs. Young hop tops, lightly steamed and served with melted butter, are delicious, and used to be sold on markets, bunched like substitute asparagus. Hops host seventeen varieties of moths, including the sword grass, ghost and twin-spotted quaker. They are a food plant of the comma, red admiral and peacock butterflies.

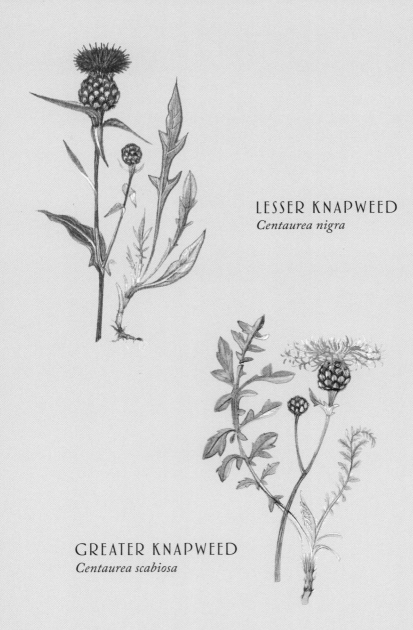

LESSER KNAPWEED
Centaurea nigra

GREATER KNAPWEED
Centaurea scabiosa

KNAPWEED

Centaurea nigra

Knapweed is a *Centaurea*, flower of the centaurs. Mythological creatures of the afterlife, half-man and half-horse, centaurs are blessed with a benevolent bent towards humans. According to legend it was Chiron, one of their number, who discovered the medicinal properties of this plant by curing a wound from a poisoned arrow shot by Hercules. From then on, knapweed was used on deep cuts, bruises, sores and scabs, and in the fourteenth century was recommended as a remedy for the plague (anything was worth a try). Sir John Hill prescribed it for bleeding and as a gargle for sore throats.

Knapweed is often known as hardheads, describing the knobby seedheads (knop or knap being archaisms for 'head'). It's a common grassland plant of roadsides and pastureland, flowering from midsummer through to late autumn. The flowers are rich in nectar and attract many insects to pollinate them, although occasionally they

> *Knapweed flowers were used by young girls for love-divination*

self-pollinate. Various *Agonopterix* moths feed on the *Centaurea* species. The solitary tufted flower-heads are a reddish-purple. *Nigra* is after the blackish scales on the involucre.

Knapweed flowers were used by young girls for love-divination, picking off the petals one by one.

158

LADY'S BEDSTRAW

Galium verum

A legend goes that the bedding where the Virgin Mary lay in childbirth was a mixture of bracken and *Galium verum*. The bracken didn't acknowledge the child when He was born, and lost its flowers, whereas the *Galium* welcomed the child joyfully and blossomed there and then. Subsequently, lady's bedstraw was the only plant in the stable the donkey didn't eat. *Verum* means true, a compliment to a faithful flower that recognised the Lord Jesus, a tradition so well known that in his painting of the Nativity, Poussin features lady's bedstraw in the manger.

The saying 'in the straw' came to mean 'in childbed', and before the days of stuffed mattresses, layers of lady's bedstraw were used instead of straw for the beds of ladies of rank, covered with a sheet. During the reign of Henry VIII lady's bedstraw was used to dye fair hair, and called maids' hair. Like sweet woodruff, which was a common strewing herb, lady's bedstraw has the most beautiful scent, sweeter than new mown hay, a delicate scent that fills a summertime room. It also has an astringency that deters fleas.

> *Before the days of stuffed mattresses, layers of lady's bedstraw were used instead of straw for the beds of ladies of rank*

William Turner had another use for it, 'preventing the sore weariness of travellers': specifically, 'the decoction of the herb and flowers, used warm, is excellent good to bath the surbated feet of footmen and lackies in hot weather, and also to lissome and mollifie the stiffness and weariness of their joynts and sinewes'. The more superstitious put lady's bedstraw into their shoes to protect them from demons.

Lady's bedstraw is a rambly perennial with linear dark green leaves set in whorls, and clusters of frothy, butter-yellow flowers. It grows in dry grassy places, on chalk downs, dry verges and heathland. It is food for fifteen moths including archer's dart, flame shoulder, hummingbird hawk-moth, small and elephant hawk-moths, and the bedstraw hawk-moth. To John Clare it was a special flower: 'I dare say a knowledge of botany woud not make me a greater lover of wild flowers then I am I love them to enthusiasm & there is many a namless flower that I lovd when a boy & worship still——I will venture to recommend 2 or 3 favorites into this garden 'Ladies bedstraw' yellow and white [G. *verum* and G. *mollugo*] are uncommonly beautiful flowers & worthy of a place any where.'

Galium comes from the Greek *gala* meaning 'milk'. As far back as Greek physician Dioscorides in the first century AD, *Galium verum* was used as a substitute for rennet in cheese-making. It contains a protein that acts as a curdling agent, and the yellow flowers give cheese a rich colour. Its honey scent when fresh led to its use by shepherds in Tuscany to give sheep's and goats' cheese a sweeter taste. Herbalist John Gerard, who grew up in Cheshire, records that it was used in making their famous cheese. One of the flower's sixteenth-century names was cheese renning, and its coagulant effect also made it useful as a styptic.

Some ancient herbalists claimed that the root, drunk in wine, is aphrodisiac, and likewise the scent of the flowers (ideal for filling a mattress, then). The roots give a red dye. In France the plant is considered to be a remedy for epilepsy; in Ireland an infusion was used on burns and skin disorders. Local names include creeping Jenny, ladies' tresses and yellow bedstraw.

Hedge bedstraw (*Galium mollugo*), its white cousin, provides food for the six-striped rustic, archer's dart, flame shoulder and hummingbird hawk, among a total of twenty moths.

LADY'S MANTLE

Alchemilla species

'Lady' plants almost always refer to the Virgin Mary, those with white flowers alluding to her purity and sanctity. Wild clematis arching over a hedgerow and offering shade to weary travellers is called lady's bower, memorialising the Flight into Egypt. Thrift is lady's cushion, harebell is lady's thimble, milk thistle is lady's thistle or blessed thistle, lady's bedstraw provided bedding for the Nativity. In the case of lady's mantle, it's the fan-like, finely toothed, pleated leaves covered in velvety down that were thought to resemble the folds of the cloak worn by Our Lady. As William Turner described the plant in 1568, 'In the night it closeth itself together like a purse, and in the morning is found full of dewe', and this dew had magical properties, of course, from being enclosed in her garment.

John Parkinson described 'the hollow crumplings and the edges also of the leaves, will containe the dew in droppes like pearles, that falleth in the night' (*Theatricum Botanicum*, 1640).

The early morning 'dew' is there even on dry days, and isn't dew at all but moisture produced by the plant itself, exuded by a process called guttation (in conditions of high humidity when water cannot be lost from the leaves as vapour,

Medieval alchemists retrieved the droplets at dawn, calling it 'celestial water' and used it in their experiments to manufacture gold from base metals

water is forced out through the breathing pores or stomata in the leaves). Medieval alchemists retrieved the droplets at dawn, calling it 'celestial water' and used it in their experiments to manufacture gold from base metals. The liquid was believed to be aphrodisiac, and was also used as an anti-wrinkle lotion. In France, lady's mantle is *herbe à la vache*, because the elf doctor appears at night with his elf bag to treat sick cows, making them sip a magic water including the 'dew', which is also sprinkled over the back and ears to cure them.

Long prized as a wound healer, Dioscorides recommended a preparation for internal and external wounds, of the root powdered and mixed with red wine. Culpeper praised it as a wound herb, and analysis shows the plant to contain tannins, a glycoside and salicylic acid. In folk medicine, an infusion of the leaves and stems was laid on greenstick fractures and broken bones in babies and young children. Lady's mantle would reverse sterility, aid conception and facilitate safe childbirth. The plant's astringent effects were sufficiently strong that it was used to contract female genitalia 'a thousand times sold' to those wishing to appear virgins. This potent substance was also said to act as a liver decongestant, and the dried flowers can be made into a pillow to help cure insomnia.

There are several native species of *Alchemilla*, perennials found on grassy roadsides and forest paths, on damp soil near ditches and on mountains. Their dense clusters of small yellowish-green flowers are the food plant of the red carpet moth. Local names include bear's foot, dew's cup, duck's foot, stellaria, lion's foot or *leontopodium*, after the spreading roots (the alchemist knew it as *pes leonis*) and elf shot. *Alchemilla*, after Arabic *Alkmelych*, means 'little alchemical one', from its apparent ability to work wonders – literally, the alchemists' plant.

LADY'S SMOCK

Cardamine pratensis

Growing in damp meadows, by streams and ditches, lady's smock is a flower of the fairies with formidable magical powers. It is not to be picked or brought into the house for fear of provoking a storm, or causing you to be struck by lightning (in France it's known as *fleur de tonnerre*). Lady's smock was used by witches in their spells, and if found in a May day garland was immediately torn to pieces because only witches picked lady's smock on 1 May. On a lighter note the flower was used, like the daisy, in love-divination by picking off the petals one by one.

April and May are when 'the cuckoo doth begin to sing her pleasant notes without stammering', as Gerard puts it. Allegedly *Cardamine pratensis* acquired its name cuckooflower because it flowers when cuckoos are first heard in spring. Alternatively, it may be because 'cuckoo-spit' (the white foam covering frog-hopper nymphs, known as spittlebugs) is often found on the leaves. It's also known as milkmaids because of its delicate, pale colouring. One quaint explanation for the name lady's smock is that the flowers look like little smocks hung out to dry, as they commonly were in early spring gardens once the weather was warm enough.

Legend has it that the mother of Constantine the Great, St Helena, found a smock in a cave near Bethlehem, left behind by Our Lady. It was later taken to St Sophia and then to Aix la Chapelle, where it was venerated for centuries. In several European countries the delicate wild flower was named in honour of the relic. Lady's smock is associated with the Feast of the Annunciation, 25 March, also known as Lady Day, which in the Gregorian calendar marked the beginning of the new year.

Lady's smock is rich in minerals and vitamins, and it's believed that where it grows abundantly the earth is rich in metals. In the old days it was sold as 'meadow bittercress' on market stalls, and people ate it in salads, or used it to cure scurvy. It was believed to attract adders, Britain's only poisonous snake, with an accompanying rural myth that anyone picking the flower would be bitten before the year was out. Lady's smock is the food plant of the orange tip butterfly and the green-veined white, and attracts numerous insects including the *Adela rufimitrella* moth. It gets its generic name *Cardamine* from two Greek words meaning 'heart' and 'to subdue', from its alleged medicinal value as a sedative; *pratensis*, 'of the meadows'. Other local names include mayflower, fairy flower and Lucy locket.

One quaint explanation for the name lady's smock is that the flowers look like little smocks hung out to dry

LESSER BURDOCK

Arctium minus

Rosalind: 'O how full of briers is this working day world!'
Celia: 'They are but burrs, cousin, thrown upon thee in holiday foolery:
if we walk not in the trodden paths, our very petticoats will catch them.'
Rosalind: 'I could shake them off my coat: these burrs are in my heart.'
Shakespeare, As You Like It

Hurr-burr, clot-burr, clouts and cockle-dock sound more like a troupe of clowns than a wild plant, but these nicknames describe the tenacious fruits of the burdock that stick to everything they latch on to, including birds whose feathers can be badly damaged by them. This sturdy weed of wayside and waste ground, with hollow stalks and heart-shaped leaves, which are woolly underneath, is the food plant of several *Lepidoptera*.

Greater burdock, *A. lappa*, a larger version, is less widely distributed throughout the British Isles, and almost absent in Wales and Ireland. Also known as sticky buttons, burdock burrs were the inspiration behind Velcro, invented by George de Mestral in the early 1940s.

Burdock has an impressive list of medicinal properties and was especially effective in easing rheumatism and joint pain: 'the seed being drunk in wine forty days together,' writes Culpeper, 'doth wonderfully help the sciatica' (or maybe it's the wine). Burdock was used for skin complaints, baldness, fevers, boils, even leprosy. Being rich in minerals and vitamins, burdock leaves are a good blood cleanser and diuretic. Highly astringent, they were used to staunch bleeding both external and internal. They can be applied to sores and ulcers, and Culpeper also recommends chewing burdock leaves to alleviate toothache.

> *Also known as Sticky Buttons, burdock burrs were the inspiration behind Velcro*

The young stalks, peeled and chopped, have an artichoke-like taste and can be put into salads, or steamed and eaten with melted butter. The tap root is popular as a vegetable in Oriental cuisines, especially in Korea and Japan. 'Dandelion and burdock' has been a popular soft drink since the Middle Ages as a non-alcoholic mead, although today the drink is more likely to contain synthesised flavouring than the fresh ingredients.

Burdock gets its name from *bur* meaning a large fruit-head, and dock from *dok*, meaning a 'stump' or bundle. *Arctium* comes from the Greek for a 'bear', burdock being a shaggy plant.

LESSER CELANDINE

Ranunculus ficaria

The lesser celandine is one of the first wild flowers to show after winter, flowering between March and May in woodland, hedgerows, on stream banks and damp pastures. 'The children call them golden daiseys', wrote John Clare of the lesser celandine: 'this is my crow flower & buttercup the childen often call them golden daiseys some of the common people know them like wise by the name of pile wort'. The plant is still known as pilewort, made into an ointment for haemorrhoids, and in Russia today, dried lesser celandine is widely sold in pharmacies as a remedy for piles (Culpeper records a medieval belief that you had only to carry it on your person for it to be effective). Golden guineas, golden stars, brighteye and starflower are other local names for this harbinger of spring that carpets the woods in 'varnish'd glory' as Tennyson put it. The glossy yellow flowers often seen with violets, which appear around the same time, shining out of tangled grass, or among old leaves under a hedge. A sun-loving member of the buttercup family, the lesser celandine closes up in the cold or in rain, opening when the sun shines and providing pollen for the *Olindia schumacherana* moth.

The generic name *Ranunculus* comes from the Latin for 'frog', after the damp habitats where the plant thrives, and *ficaria* describes the knotted tubers, which resemble a bunch of figs (or piles). They reminded farmers of cows' teats, so they hung them up in the cowshed to ensure a rich supply of creamy milk – acquiring for the flower names of butter-and-cheese, and cream-and-butter. Lesser celandine is known in some localities as scurvywort, since the high vitamin content in the leaves cured vitamin C deficiency: the leaves were boiled and eaten like spinach, or put into salads raw, and the flower-buds pickled as a substitute for capers.

> *Also known as Golden Stars and starflower, it was Wordsworth's favourite flower*

In the language of flowers lesser celandine, the first flower to arrive after our British winter, stands for 'joys to come'. It was Wordsworth's favourite flower, and he requested that it be carved on his gravestone. Unfortunately the stonemason got it wrong and put the greater celandine there instead: poor Wordsworth, deprived of his favourite flower for eternity.

LORDS AND LADIES

Arum maculatum

The wavy-edged leaves of *Arum maculatum* push up through the ground in late winter, often in deep shade. Within a few weeks, arum's arrow-shaped spathe unfurls to reveal a plant famous for its phallic imagery. Cuckoopint, as it's widely known, derives from the cuckoo as harbinger of spring, but also an Old English word *pintel* for the male member. Many of its vernacular names echo the phallic association: Adam and Eve, bulls and cows, men and women, kings and queens, stallions and mares. By association with its distinctive shape, Dioscorides claimed it was aphrodisiac: 'it is uretical too, and stirs up affections to conjunction being drank with wine'. Its inherent symbolism of fertility wins it a place on the Unicorn Tapestries, woven in 1514 as a wedding gift for King François I of France and his wife Claude, Duchess of Brittany.

Arum also has nicknames of Jack-(or parson- or man-)in-the-pulpit, and in *Far From the Madding Crowd* Thomas Hardy describes the plant as 'an apoplectic saint in a niche of malachite'.

Growing in hedgerows, woodland and gardens, England's wild passion flower of late winter is also called starchwort and arrowroot. The tuberous roots contain a floury substance used as a substitute for arrowroot and called Portland sago, extracted on the Isle of Portland. Arum's starch was also used to stiffen Elizabethan and Jacobean ruffs, but was hard on the hands: 'The most pure and white starch is made of the roots of Cuckowpint; but most hirtful to the hands of the Laundresse that hath the handling of it, for it choppeth, blistereth and maketh the hands rough and rugged, and withal smarting', writes Gerard in his 1597 *Herbal*. Powdered and mixed with rose water, the starch was made into a face-cream to whiten the skin and improve the complexion, and was popular with the Elizabethans. John Pechey, seventeenth-century herbalist, wrote that 'women do use the distilled water of the root to beautify their faces; but the juice of the root, set in the sun, is much better'.

> *Thomas Hardy describes the plant as 'an apoplectic saint in a niche of malachite'*

John Clare notes how, in spring, 'the hedge bottoms are crowded with the green leaves of the arum ... there are 2 sorts wild here one bright green & another darker spotted with jet'. He describes a late winter's ramble '... before the arum dare peep out of its hood or the primrose & violet shoot up a new leaf thro the warm moss & ivy that shelter their spring dwellings'. The pale green hooded spathe of lords and ladies contains either a purple (*Arum maculatum*) or yellow (*Arum italicum*) poker-like spadix. At the base are clustered, deep inside, a ring of female flowers (the 'ladies') and another of male (the 'lords') flowers. The unfurling spadix emits a foul smell attracting small flies known as owl-midges. They penetrate the sheath, often in their hundreds, pollinating the female flower. The resulting bright red berries appearing on the spike in July and August are poisonous, and other parts of the fresh plant can cause allergic reactions, although the root is edible and nutritious if it's well baked. The generic name *Arum* comes from a Greek word for poisonous plants, and *maculatum* means 'spotted', describing the purple blotches on the leaves, hence another local name, spotted wake Robin.

> *Unclos'd the arum leaves and into view*
> *Its ear-like spindling flowers their cases burst*
> JOHN CLARE, ON THE SIGHT OF SPRING

LUNGWORT
Pulmonaria officinalis

A member of the borage family, lungwort creates pools of azure in woods and hedgerows from March to May. Native to central Europe, it's also a widely cultivated perennial, which escapes back into its wild habitat. The leaves are covered in tiny coarse hairs rough to the touch, and the flowers may initially be pink, turning an intense violet-blue, hence its many double names like soldiers-and-sailors, Josephs and Marys, Adam and Eve. The white spots on the leaves were where drops of the Virgin's milk, or the Virgin's tears at the Crucifixion, fell on to the plant, hence a local name of Jerusalem cowslip. Gerard recommended the leaves as a culinary herb, calling it spotted comfrey, and sage of Jerusalem.

With their white speckles the leaves were thought to resemble lung tissue, and by sympathetic magic were a cure 'against the infirmities and ulcers of the lungs'. As it turns out, in days when wild plants were the local pharmacy, lungwort proved an effective treatment for chronic bronchitis, and was combined with coltsfoot for

The white spots on the leaves were where drops of the Virgin's milk, or the Virgin's tears at the Crucifixion, fell on to the plant

persistent coughs. The leaves contain mucilage and high levels of silicic acid, allantoin, flavonoids and tannins and vitamin C. Although nowadays used only in homeopathy for bronchitis and for oral and throat infections, lungwort's leaves are astringent and can be used to stop bleeding, and an herbal infusion of the dried leaves can make a perfectly safe gargle for coughs and laryngitis.

MALLOW

Common mallow (Malva sylvestris)
Musk mallow (Malva moschata)

A wayside plant also found on beaches and waste ground, common mallow has velvet-soft leaves and a jewel-like amethyst flower. The musk mallow is a paler mauve, and has a musky scent. This wild flower was once grown not just for its ravishing flowers but as a culinary herb, prized as a vegetable as well as for valuable medicinal properties. As a result, in the language of flowers mallow came to stand for beneficence. Theophrastus recommended mallow as a cough remedy, and the Greeks and Romans cultivated it for the leaves as a vegetable: both flowers and leaves are very good in salads and are rich in vitamins A, B1, B2 and C. The poet Martial used mallow to dispel hangovers after orgies (although Cicero complained it gave him indigestion). Aristophanes writes of 'eating mallow shoots instead of loaves of wheat', and Horace in his Odes wrote 'I fed on olives, endives and light mallows'. Mallow has a place in Chinese cuisine, and many country children knew the flat round seeds as 'cheeses', eating them raw, or steamed in salads for their nutty flavour. John Clare recalls:

> The sitting down, when school was o'er
> Upon the threshold of the door
> Picking from Mallows sport 'to please
> The crumpled seed we call a cheese.

Some claimed mallow to be aphrodisiac, and Pythagoras recommended it for 'moderating the passions and clearing the stomach and mind', although generally speaking in the Middle Ages it had a reputation as an anti-aphrodisiac, promoting calm and sober conduct.

Its medicinal uses were many. Pliny wrote: 'whosoever shall take a spoonful of any of the mallows shall that day be free from all the diseases that may come unto him'. *Hortus Sanitatis* of 1435 claims the leaves would draw out the stings of wasps, and a draught of musk mallow roots boiled with raisins should be bottled and taken as an early-morning potion to protect against disease. Sixteenth-century herbalists and simplers regarded the plant as a cure-all: internally it was used as a purgative and laxative, externally as an ointment for soothing swellings and insect bites. 'Sodden with vinegar and linseed', goes one recipe; it was an antidote to 'the wicked gatherings that be engendered in a man's body'. Moreover it kept witches away from the house.

The dried roots of musk mallow are still sold by chemists in France where they are given to babies to chew on while teething, and to soothe the stomach. The healing mucilage was also made into poultices, ointments and a syrup for sore throats and bronchitis. Fresh roots contain a thick white gelatinous substance from which marshmallows used to be made (today they are made from gelatine, sugar, water and egg whites). The plant also yields a fibre for fabric, and Muhammad was so delighted with a robe of mallow that he transformed the flower, so goes the legend, into a pelargonium.

Perhaps the strangest use for mallow was devised to test the innocence of a suspected criminal: an early lie-detector test made the suspect hold a red-hot iron. It was found that the mucilage of marsh mallow combined with the seeds of fleabane and the white of an

> *The poet Martial used mallow to dispel hangovers after orgies*

egg, made into a paste and rubbed over the hand, modified the heat and would enable an innocent person to hold the glowing metal for a few moments without injury.

Malva comes from the Greek *malakos*, meaning 'soft' or emollient, from its mucilaginous quality and soft leaves; *Sylvestris*, 'of the woods'. Marsh mallow (*Althaea officinalis*) is the most medicinally effective of the group, as implied by its specification: *althos* is Greek for 'remedy,' and *officinalis* means a medicinal herb. Common mallow (*Malva sylvestris*) is a food plant of the least yellow underwing, mallow and hollyhock seed moths, and for the painted lady butterfly. Local names include bread and cheese, Billy buttons, cheeses, fairy cheeses and rags and tatters. In Norfolk it is pick-cheese, and in French *herbe à fromage*.

MEADOWSWEET

Filipendula ulmaria

'Queen of the meadow' in many languages, meadowsweet has a long history as a medicinal plant. Salicylic acid isolated from meadowsweet was first synthesised in the 1890s to make acetylsalicylic acid, later known as aspirin. At the time, the plant was classified as a *Spiraea*, from which the name aspirin derives. A tea of the flowers is diaphoretic, long used in the treatment of colds, fevers and influenza. The creamy flowers also contain flavonoids and tannins, which with other essential oils in the plant act to protect the lining of the stomach and intestine (unlike aspirin which can cause gastric ulceration), so are an effective remedy for hyperacidity and heartburn. As well as a cure for acid indigestion, meadowsweet alleviates joint problems, the salicylates helping to reduce inflammation and relieve arthritic pain and rheumatism (for which it was famed in folk medicine). The root is employed specifically as a safe remedy for diarrhoea, even in children, and you can chew a piece of the root to relieve a headache. The plant is also diuretic and a remedy for fluid retention, and being antiseptic it has an effect on urinary tract infections. It was used as a kidney and bladder tonic, employed along with other herbs in irritable bowels, and occasionally for cystitis.

> *It was said to be Queen Elizabeth I's favourite scent, 'for the smell thereof maketh the hart merrie'*

The sweet fragrance of meadowsweet is much used in pot-pourri and sachets, and was a welcome strewing herb in medieval and Tudor times. It was said to be Queen Elizabeth I's favourite scent, 'for the smell thereof maketh the hart merrie, delighteth the senses: neither doth it cause headache, or lothsomnesse to meate, as some other sweete smelling herbes do', as Gerard records. It was a particularly popular strewing herb at weddings, and was put into bridal garlands to promote love, hence a local name of bridewort.

In folklore, the sweet scent has the power to grant second sight and an ability to converse with the fairies. But it had its sinister side too: in excess, the scent could be nauseating, and over the centuries there were reports that children with bunches of meadowsweet in their bedrooms were found insensible in the morning. It was regarded as a fatal flower in Wales, and it was thought dangerous to fall asleep in a field of meadowsweet because too much of the scent would cause fits. In some parts it was believed unlucky in the house and associated with death. Certainly it makes a mess indoors: the tiny petals fall easily, and pollen dust goes everywhere. One local name is old man's pepper, the old man in question being the Devil.

Meadowsweet was one of the most sacred herbs of the Druids. It has many practical uses: with a copper mordant it yields a black dye;

the leaves were a popular flavouring for soup; and the flowers make a herbal tea. Meadowsweet was used to flavour beer before hops arrived in Britain; the dried flowers used to be smoked like tobacco; and Culpeper recommends infusing them in claret for their perfume. In Ireland meadowsweet was used to scour milk churns.

A perennial, meadowsweet flowers between June and September on riverbanks, in wet meadows and along damp hedgerows, in ditches, on fen and marshland. Its foam of cream flowers contains no nectar but attracts insects to their abundant, sweet-scented pollen, providing a food source for seventeen moths including the emperor moth and the wonderfully named setaceous Hebrew character, the lesser cream wave and glaucous shears moths.

Local names include hayriff, kiss-me-quick, lady of the meadow, sweet hay, tea flower, bride of the meadow, new mown hay and meadow-queen. In France it is *reine de prés*. Chaucer mentions it in 'The Knight's Tale' as meadwort, and Gerard calls it medeswete. Before him William Turner, in 1568, had named it medewurte, since it was widely used to flavour mead. *Filipendula* comes from two Latin words meaning 'thread' and 'hanging', describing the fibrous roots, and *ulmaria* means 'elm-like': not that meadowsweet is remotely elm-like to look at, but slippery elm bark contains salicylic acid too, and was as common a painkiller as the 'queen of the meadow'.

MILKWORT

Polygala vulgaris

Widely distributed across Britain, milkwort favours chalk and limestone and is found on heathland, dunes, moor and grassland. The enchanting spikes of flowers have two oversized sepals of a celestial blue (or sometimes white, mauve or pink), which cradle the inner flower. The eight stamens fuse into a tube, with two tiny petals on each side and a larger third petal, delicately fringed, underneath. The beautiful milkwort is a perennial, flowering from May to September, and is a food plant of the small purple-barred moth. The stem exudes a milky white sap when cut, hence the common name.

In Wales, milkwort is known as Christ's herb, since it comes into flower around Ascension Day. Other names include fairy soap (in Donegal they believed fairies made a lather from the roots and leaves, and indeed a crude soap can be obtained much like that of soapwort or *Saponaria*, but less effective). Milkwort is also known as four sisters (from the different colours in the flowers) and Mother Mary's milk.

Milkwort used to be woven into garlands to carry in Rogation Day processions, and has a host of Rogation-tide names: procession flower, cross-flower, rogation flower and gang-flower (after an old English word for 'going' or walking). Over four days before Ascension Day in May, the parish boundaries are walked ('beating the bounds') and the crops blessed by a priest of the diocese, invoking protection against plague, fires and wild beasts. A processional Cross is carried, hence cross-flower, and bells rung 'that demons may flee in terror'.

In Wales, milkwort is known as Christ's Herb, since it comes into flower around Ascension Day

Milkwort's botanical name comes from the *polugalon* or 'much milk' of Dioscorides, and in many herbals the plant is said to encourage the production of milk in nursing mothers. This galactagogue attribute is unsubstantiated, but milkwort has proved valuable for the treatment of respiratory problems: it was used to treat chest complaints, even serious ones like pleurisy, chronic bronchitis, asthma and whooping cough. Milkwort's close relative *P. senega* or Seneca snakeroot, named after the Seneca tribe of North America who used it for snake bites, was highly valued by the Native Indians and early settlers as an expectorant for respiratory disorders, and was also sweat-inducing, diuretic and, in large doses, emetic.

TUFTED MILKWORT
Polygala comosa

HEATH MILKWORT
Polygala serpyllifolia

MUGWORT

Artemisia vulgaris

Eldest of worts
Thou hast might for three
And against thirty,
For venom availest
For flying things,
Mighty 'gainst loathed ones
That through the land rove.

FROM THE *LACNUNGA*, ANGLO-SAXON HERBAL

Mugwort is Queen of herbs, named after the moon goddess Artemis, huntress of the forests, mother-goddess whose temple at Ephesus was one of the Seven Wonders of the ancient world. *Artemesia* leaves found their way out of pagan folklore into medieval stonecarving, and along with oak and maple they can be found on cathedral capitals in Exeter among other places. From the earliest days mugwort was a herb for travellers: Dioscorides wrote that 'If any have ye herb Artemesia with him in ye way, it dissolves weariness and he that

> *A sleep pillow of dried mugwort protected you from nightmares and would give you prophetic dreams*

bears it on his feet, drives away venomous beasts and devils.' Roman centurions wore it in their shoes to keep the soles of the feet in good shape, and maybe there was something in the idea since it persisted into the seventeenth century: in 1656 in *The Art of Simpling* William Coles wrote, 'If a footman take mugwort and put it in his shoes in the morning, he may goe forty miles before noon and not be weary.'

Mugwort was one of the nine magical herbs used to combat witchcraft and evil, as powerful as St John's Wort and used in many of the same ways, including in garlands hung over doorways and windows as protection from bad spirits. *The Grete Herball* states, 'Yf this herbe be within a house there shall no wycked spyryte abyde.' Stockmen who put mugwort into stables found that even the most intractable animals became manageable. In Japan, bunches of mugwort exorcised spirits that caused illness. A sleep pillow of dried mugwort protected you from nightmares and would give you prophetic dreams, and if you placed a fresh sprig of mugwort under the pillow you would able to divine them.

Medicinally, mugwort was something of a cure-all:

> *If they would drink nettles in March*
> *And eat mugwort in May*
> *So many fine maidens*
> *Wouldn't go to the clay.*

Its uses included a cure for fevers, consumption and other lung complaints. The bitter taste was used to stimulate appetite and soothe indigestion, as an antispasmodic to ease period pains, and even to stop haemorrhaging in childbirth. A reliable relaxant for anxiety and tension, mugwort has a long history as a vermifuge and is renowned as an insect-repellent: the Old Saxon *muggia wort* means midge-plant, from its deterrent effect on flies and moths. In Chinese medicine it's known as moxa: the leaves, dried and powdered, are pounded into sticks and burned near the skin to stimulate meridian energies.

Mugwort was used to flavour drinks, especially beer, and was put into savoury stuffings for roast birds, traditionally goose. It was also mixed into the feed of turkeys and other poultry to fatten them for the table. If however livestock graze on it, it taints their milk, and in Switzerland mugwort has been known to have poisoned cattle. The flowers and stems yield a green dye, and country people made the leaves into a herbal tobacco. With its cousin *Artemisia campestris* it is a food plant for the mullein wave, mouse, mugwort plume and diamond pearl moths, among over twenty in total.

Maverick author and botanist Sir John Hill, whose life spanned the eighteenth century and whose provocative and scurrilous writings involved him in many quarrels, has full confidence in mugwort. Championing plant medicine he wrote, 'The leaves and tops of the younge shootes and flowers in this plant are all full of virtue, they are aromatic to the taste and with a little sharpness. The herb has been famous from the earliest times, and providence has placed it everywhere about our doors so that reason, and authority, as well as the notice of our senses, point it out for use, but chemistry has banished natural medicine.'

MULLEIN

Aaron's rod (Verbascum thapsus)
Dark mullein (Verbascum nigrum)

A dramatic, stately flower with spikes of bright yellow petals progressing up a stem to the height of a tall man, mullein grows throughout England and Wales. It rises out of a rosette of basal leaves a foot long and covered in dense silvery-green hairs. These gold sentries host many insects including halictid bees and hoverflies, some species of bees using the hairs in the making of their nests. Mullein thrives in a variety of habitats from rough grassland to hedgerows, roadsides to waste ground, although rarely in the north of Britain. It prefers chalky and sandy soils, and needs disturbed ground for the prolific seeds to germinate (one spike can produce up to 240,000 seeds). Flowering from June to August, mulleins are insect-pollinated or self-pollinated. Belonging to the same family as

foxgloves, they contain
poisonous glycosides that
can cause death to animals,
although generally
livestock avoid them.

Farmers take care that neither are included in hay.

The flowering stems were once used as tapers: Henry Lyte, writing in 1578, says 'The whole toppe with its plesant yellow floures sheweth like to a wax candle or taper cunningly wrought.' After being dried, the spike was dipped in tallow and burned to give light at outdoor gatherings, hence a local name of high taper. The Romans called them *candelaria*, or *candela regia*, and used them to light lanterns and as tapers to burn at funerals. Until the nineteenth-century Industrial Revolution, before cotton was widely available in Britain, the downy covering of mullein leaves was gathered and used to make into wicks for lamps, and at country gatherings the entire stem was burned as a flare. The thick, downy leaves have a pleasant fruity smell when crushed, and were once used by the poor to line their shoes in winter to keep feet warm: fragrant insoles. Dried, the leaves were mixed into herbal tobaccos; the flowers yield dyes of bright to pale yellow, which have been used as hair colouring; and the whole plant looks stunning in a flower border. Great mullein (*Verbascum thapsus*) is a food plant for the *Paratalanta hyalinalis* moth.

In folk medicine, those leaves in your shoes would help prevent you from catching colds, and regular consumption of a small amount of mullein was supposed to ensure a long life. It was considered magical as well as medicinal, although Gerard had his doubts: 'There be some who think that this herbe being carryed aboute one, doth helpe the falling sicknesse ... which thing is vaine and superstitious', but he did recommend it as a cough medicine. Country people would smoke the dried leaves in a clay pipe for bronchitis and asthma, and for good reason: since ancient times, mullein has had a place in authentic medicine for throat and breathing ailments, as well as skin complaints. Dioscorides recommended it for diseases of the lungs, and two thousand years later it is still available in health and herbal stores. Pliny concurred, and analysis shows mullein to contain mucilage, flavonoids, tannins, saponins and glycosides. It is emollient, weakly sedative, expectorant, anti-inflammatory, antiviral, antibacterial and analgesic. The leaves and flowers, infused, can be given for sore throats and coughs, and a syrup made for the treatment of croup. Being emollient and a good wound-healer, mullein can be used externally: a poultice of the powdered root was applied to sores, rashes and skin infections, and an infusion of the root for athlete's foot. In Germany, the flowers are steeped in olive oil and used for ear infections and haemorrhoids, and this oil has been proved effective for eczema, catarrh, colic, earache, frostbite, warts, boils, carbuncles and chilblains. The flowers are rich in mucilage with potential anti-tumour agents, and made into a tea (combining well with coltsfoot) can relieve coughs and colds, act as a diuretic and ease rheumatic pain.

Ulysses carried this magical herb of the ancients to shield him from the powers of Circe: 'and he after that dreaded none of her evil works ... If a man beareth with him one twig of this wort, he will not be terrified with any awe, nor will a wild beast hurt him; or any evil coming near' or so it says in the *Herbarium* of Apuleius Platonicus. Subsequently, simply carrying mullein was supposed to ward off wild beasts, curses and evil spirits. Witches used mullein tapers to light nocturnal meetings, they used the plant in their incantations and spells, and it provided them with broomsticks. Mullein became known as hag taper after this belief, although *hag* is also an old English word for hedge. Other names include Aaron's flannel, blanket mullein, candlewick plant, feltwort, lamb's ear, velvet mullein, Jupiter's staff, torches and

Country people would smoke the dried leaves in a clay pipe for bronchitis and asthma

figwort, because figs were stored between mullein leaves to keep them moist and soft. In Italy it's known as light of the Lord, in other places as Virgin Mary's candle or Mary's taper. In the USA it acquired the name cowboy toilet paper!

In the USA it acquired the name Cowboy Toilet Paper!

Most widely known as Aaron's rod, its staff-like appearance gives rise to its commonest name: the rod of Levi on which Aaron's name was inscribed produced buds and blossoms when it was placed in the Tabernacle. In the Book of Numbers (17:8), Moses gives the princes of Israel a rod each, a symbol of power: 'And Moses laid up the rods before the Lord in the tabernacle of witness. And it came to pass, on the morrow Moses went into the tabernacle of witness; and behold, the rod of Aaron for the house of Levi was budded and brought forth buds, and bloomed blossoms.'

Mullein's specific name *thapsus* was first coined by Theophrastus for an unspecified herb from the Ancient Greek settlement of Thapsos, near modern day Syracuse. Mullein derives from *mollis* meaning 'soft', after the leaves – hence local names like donkey's ears, bunny's ears and bull's ears. *Verbascum* means 'bearded', after the hairy leaves.

GREAT MULLEIN
Verbascum thapsus

MOTH MULLEIN
Verbascum blattaria

192

NETTLE

Urtica dioica

Atextile plant from ancient times, the heart-fibre of the nettle makes the strongest natural thread known to man: however, since 40kg of wild nettles are needed to make a single shirt they were eventually displaced by hemp and flax. Nettle's cultural history stretches from a Bronze Age grave in Denmark where scraps of nettle cloth were found wrapped around cremated bones, to a trade in nettles from England to towns of the Hanseatic League, to the Second World War when the bast fibre was used in the manufacture of parachutes and ropes. In eighteenth-century Scotland nettles were woven into linen-like sheets and tablecloths, and in France made into paper. The nineteenth-century poet Thomas Campbell wrote, 'I have slept in Nettle sheets, and I have dined off a Nettle tablecloth. The young and tender nettle is an excellent pot-herb, and the stalks of the old nettle are as good as flax for making cloth. I have heard my mother say, she thought Nettle cloth more durable than any other.' Hans Christian Andersen's princess wove nettlecloth coats for her seven swans without speaking while she did so, to magic them back into human form.

> *The heart-fibre of the nettle makes the strongest natural thread known to man*

Growing across northern Europe and throughout Asia and North America, nettles grow freely on riverbanks and ditches, in farms and gardens, on rubbish tips and fire sites, in woodland and on wasteland. They are frequently found around abandoned buildings: a colony of nettles indicates fertile soil and is often a clue to a long-disappeared midden. Nettles thrive in phosphorous-rich earth, stimulating the formation of humus and leaving it rich and workable. They start showing as soon as winter is over, flowering from June to August, and are wind-pollinated. Host to the black and white caterpillar of the peacock butterfly, stinging nettles are the food plant of the comma, map, red admiral and small tortoiseshell butterflies, and to no less than three dozen beautiful moths, including the mother of pearl, small magpie, white ermine and angle shades. Some birds make use of nettles for nesting sites: John Clare noted that 'Small whitethroat [lesser whitethroat] builds a nest of materials ... it chuses low clumps of brambles near the ground & I have often found it in beds of the keen nettle curiously fixed between them.'

> *In eighteenth-century Scotland nettles were woven into linen-like sheets*

Nettles were exported to America by the Pilgrim Fathers, where they naturalised. Rich in iron, potassium, manganese, calcium and nitrogen, they contain protein, formic acid, vitamins A and C and other mineral salts. Nettles are the gardener's friend: added to compost they put nitrogen back into the soil and are an active accelerator in decomposition. You can make your own insecticide for aphids and blackfly by soaking nettles in rainwater for several days, and this can also be used as a liquid fertiliser rich in iron, magnesium and sulphur. Pack fruit in nettles to preserve their bloom, and grow nettles near root vegetables to improve their storing qualities. Let nettles grow near roses and the roses will thrive.

This amazing plant has a multitude of everyday uses. Nettle juice curdles milk and was used in the past instead of rennet in the production of Cheshire cheese, and to flavour Gouda. Nettles have been used for commercial supplies of chlorophyll, and the plant yields green and yellow dyes. Nettle oil preceded paraffin for lighting lamps. A bunch of nettles hung in the larder repels flies, and near beehives they drive away frogs. Nettles even have cosmetic uses: nettle juice combed through the hair was recommended as a cure for baldness, for dandruff, and as a hairwash to improve the colour and glossiness of hair. For this reason some farmers include a handful of nettles with cattle feed. Dried nettle leaves ground into chicken feed increases egg-production.

Nettles were one of the five bitter herbs eaten at Passover. Nettle tea, having a high vitamin-C content, is renowned as a spring tonic and there was a street-vendors' cry: 'Nettles with tender shoots to cleanse the blood.' In country medicine, an infusion of nettles made a good gargle, and nettle tea, which is diuretic and prescribed for kidney trouble, was found to ease colds, sore throats and catarrh, bronchitis and asthma. It was found to reduce blood-sugar levels and its iron content was useful in cases of anaemia and bleeding. 'He that holdeth this herbe in hys hand with an herbe called Mylfoyle (yarrow), for noseblede, is sure from all feare and fantasye or vysion', declares *The Boke of Secrets*, an anonymous sixteenth-century compilation claiming the authorship of Albertus Magnus, twelfth-century Dominican theologian and philosopher.

Nettles make a surprisingly delicious springtime soup, and a purée of nettles can provide a spinach-like base for poached eggs. Pepys wrote in 1661, 'We did eat some nettle porridge, which was made on purpose today for some of their coming, and was very good' (nettle porridge is made by adding the cooked leaves – boiling them neutralises the sting – to oats and melted butter). Nettle beer is easy to make and was a popular rustic drink. In his *Herbal* of 1597 Gerard claims that 'nettles baked with sugar make the vital spirits more fresh and lively'.

John Clare called it the 'keen nettle', likening the sting to ant bites: 'these little things are armd with stings that blister & torture the skin with a pain worse then the keen nettle'. The sting contains corrosive formic acid, causing severe irritation: rhubarb leaves contain an antidote, and so do mint, rosemary and sage, but above all, as the country saying goes:

Nettle out, dock in
Dock remove the nettle sting.

In Clare's day there was a popular belief that nettle stings were a remedy for rheumatism, from lore going back to early times when nettle stings were thought to stimulate the entire human organism. Children who got stung all over their legs were told they would be healthy for the rest of their lives, and would never suffer from rheumatism. The Romans went so far as to cultivate nettles so that they could use them for 'urtication', whipping with nettles, to cure not only rheumatism but also typhoid fever and apoplectic fits. They rubbed themselves vigorously with nettles in the winter to warm chilled limbs. The leaves contain several chemicals including histamine, serotonin and formic acid, and are processed in Germany for the treatment of arthritis, since they have been found to protect synovial fluid in the joints. Maybe Hildegard von Bingen knew something we don't: in her twelfth-century *Physica*, she suggests nettle preparations as a treatment for senility: 'And a person who is unwillingly forgetful should pound stinging nettle to a juice, and add a bit of olive oil. When he goes to bed, he should thoroughly anoint his chest and temples with it. If he does this often, forgetfulness will diminish.'

In Germany, nettles are consecrated to Thor, guardian deity of marriage, and nettle seed was believed to 'excite the passions'. In Denmark, nettle clumps were believed to grow where innocent blood had been shed, and in Yorkshire nettles were used to exorcise the devil. Nettle beds are the homes of elves, so nettle stings defend you from sorcery, and a bunch of nettles hung in the dairy protected the milk from witches' spells. In many places it was thought that nettles worn on the person in times of danger drove away fear, inspired courage and protected from evil spirits. A thunder-plant, if you threw it on the fire during a storm it would protect the house from lightning.

In medieval symbolism the nettle stands for envy, in flower language for slander and cruelty, on account of its sting. To dream of being stung by nettles means disappointment and vexation, but to dream of gathering nettles means that someone has formed a favourable opinion of you. If you are married it means your family will be blessed with harmony and concord.

Aesop offers this proverb:

> Tender-handed stroke a nettle
> And it stings you for its pains
> Grasp it like a man of mettle
> And it soft as silk remains.

Nettles have spawned shrewd observations on life: 'Though you stroke the nettle ever so kindly, yet it will sting you' and 'He that handles a nettle tenderly is soonest stung'. 'Grasp the nettle' is a well-known exhortation. In German, to 'sit in nettles' means to get into trouble, and nettles provided Sir Thomas Browne with this reflection:

> Such is the posies Love composes:
> A stinging nettle mixed with Roses

Nettle's common name comes from an ancient root *ned*, 'to twist', referring to its fibre. Its generic name derives from the Latin *uro*, 'to burn' or sting. *Dioica* means dioecious, bearing male and female flowers on separate plants (*dis* means double, *oikos* house). The Anglo-Saxon *netel* is the same root as *noedl* or needle, from the pricking sting. Local names include Devil's leaf, Devil's plaything, naughty man's plaything, hidgy-pidgy, hoky-poky, tanging nettle, burn nettle and burn weed.

PERIWINKLE

Vinca major, V. minor

Chaucer loved this bewitching flower, with its blue dazzle, 'fresshe pervinke, rich of hue'. With its five violet-blue petals borne on a single stem, and glossy evergreen leaves making thick ground-cover, periwinkle was the 'joy of the ground' to the medievals. Native to southern Europe and North Africa, it was probably introduced by the Romans to Britain, where it naturalised. In 1551 William Turner wrote that periwinkle 'groweth ... wylde ... in the west cuntre'. Periwinkle grows in hedgerows and copses and is often found in ancient woodland. *Vinca minor* is pollinated by bee-flies and bumblebees, *V. major* by long-tongued bumblebees, and the orange tip butterfly nectars on the flowers.

Periwinkle was believed to be endowed with magical powers, and in France is still the sorcerer's violet, *violette des sorciers*. 'Whoever carries this herb with him on the skin, the devil has no power over him', states *Hortus Sanitatis* of 1491. 'No witchery may enter the house which has this herb hanging over the door and if any witchery be already therein it will be driven out soon. With this herb wicked spirits are cast out of people ... and it works much better if the herb is blessed with other herbs on Lady Day.' The flower became a symbol of friendship, and if you dream of periwinkle it means that a spirit watches over you.

> *If you dream of periwinkle it means that a spirit watches over you*

In Italy, periwinkle is *fiore di morte*, flower of death, because heretics were led to the stake wearing periwinkle garlands. Simon Frazer wore one on his way to execution at the Tower of London in 1306 after the overthrow of William Wallace. These garlands were placed on funeral biers of children, too, the evergreen periwinkle being a symbol of immortality. Sometimes periwinkle was planted on children's graves, and it was unlucky to uproot them because you would either be haunted by the ghost of the deceased, or suffer from nightmares.

Periwinkle has always been known as a powerful medicinal herb, and nowadays vincristine and vinblastine, alkaloids extracted from *V. rosea*, are used in chemotherapy to treat leukemias, lymphomas and childhood cancers. *Vinca minor* contains the alkaloid vincamin, used in pharmaceutical preparations as a cerebral stimulant and vasodilator, stimulating blood flow to the brain and inner ears. This was familiar to practitioners of folk medicine who found that it improved brain function and memory. They also used periwinkle in the treatment of haemorrhaging, in diabetes, as a hypotensive drug and a sedative. Its styptic properties were used to bind open wounds (in Devon its local name is cut finger), and chewing the leaves would stop a bleeding tooth cavity. Sir Francis Bacon claimed that you could prevent cramp in the leg by binding periwinkle leaves around it. It would also 'stay the flux, ease the toothache and drive out the wicked fever that comes of severe cold'.

In Italy, periwinkle is fiore di morte, flower of death, because heretics were led to the stake wearing periwinkle garlands

Gerard makes a characteristically unsupported claim that 'the young tops made into a conserve is good for the nightmare'. Culpeper, however, considers the periwinkle aphrodisiac: 'Venus owns this herb, and saith, that the leaves eaten by a Man and his Wife together, cause love between them.' In the alchemical *Boke of Secrets*, attributed in the 1600s to Albertus Magnus, it is revealed that 'periwynke beat into a powder with wormes of the earth wrapped about it and with an herbe called horeslyke [houseleek?], it induceth love between man and wife ... if it bee used with their meals.... If dried perwynke be placed between where two lovers lie, there will be no strife or malice between them', so the fact that periwinkle features on the Unicorn Tapestries of 1514, alongside other flowers of fertility, comes as no surprise.

Periwinkle gets its name from the Medieval Latin *pervincula*, *per* meaning 'throughout', and *vincio* 'bind'. It binds itself to the ground by putting down roots from nodes on the trailing stems. Variously pervenke, parvink, pervinke from the Old French *pervenche*, in Italian periwinkle is *centocchio* or a hundred eyes, named for the numerous bright flowers among dark leaves. In England, periwinkle has local names of blue buttons, penny winkle, cockles and sorcerer's violet.

LESSER
PERIWINKLE
Vinca minor

PRIMROSE

Primula vulgaris

Among thy woodland shady nooks
The primrose wanly comes.
JOHN CLARE

The primrose is the 'first rose' of spring, symbol of Easter's new life. Its pale flowers light up damp, shady places in deciduous woodland, sprinkling grassy banks and hedgerows from March to May, although John Clare wrote of finding them even earlier: 'Winter Primroses––I have gathered a handful of primrose in hilly wood on christmass day in the midst of a severe frost not only once but many years.' In folklore they are a symbol of youth, and believed to be lucky in love and marriage, although they have their darker side too: the famous 'primrose path of dalliance' spoken by

Ophelia in *Hamlet* has gone into common parlance, and a porter in *Macbeth* mutters, 'I had thought to have let in some of all professions, that go the primrose way to the everlasting bonfire.'

Hang a bunch of primroses in the cowshed and your cattle will be protected from evil spirits. Small bunches left on the doorstep on the eve of May Day, when witches are active, will repel them. In the old days, both petals and leaves were used in salads, and people said that eating primroses made the invisible visible, or that children who did were given powers to see fairies. Pull the petals off a primrose one by one and you will discover whether 'he loves me or he loves me not'. Primroses were said to bloom in Paradise, and if you found one with exactly six leaves, you would have good luck in affairs of the heart.

In folklore they are a symbol of youth, and believed to be lucky in love and marriage

In Germany, a primrose is key flower, *Erdschlüsselblume*, because it was believed it could dowse hidden treasure and open locks. In parts of England it was considered unlucky to bring fewer than 13 primroses into the house when picking the first posy of spring: an old wives' tale went that if you did, the number you brought in would equal the number of eggs each of your hens would hatch during the entire year. If you took just one indoors, only a single chick would hatch out of the brood (in some places this would happen to your geese). Bringing a lone primrose into the house was unlucky because it heralded a death in the family, and in Shakespeare's *Cymbeline* it was a funeral flower for youth:

> With fairest flowers
> Whilst summer last, and I live here, Fidele,
> I'll sweeten thy sad grave: thou shalt not lack
> The flower that's like thy face, pale primrose.

Country wives used to make primrose tea to ease rheumatism, arthritis and migraine. An infusion of the flower-heads was a general blood-cleanser in the spring, and a non-addictive cure for insomnia – even just putting a primrose on your pillow would help. The Romans used primroses against malaria and jaundice, and medieval herbalists made typically optimistic claims that primroses could cure all manner of ills from 'frenzie' to the King's Evil. Gerard's 1597 *Herbal* claimed that 'the roots of primrose stamped and strained and the juice sniffed into the nose with a quill purge the braine'. In Lincolnshire, a decoction of the leaves was prescribed for failing memory, and in Wales primrose juice was a cure for madness. Soaked in vinegar, the flowers were a cure for scrofula, a form of tuberculosis of the neck. An ointment for chilblains was made by boiling the flowers in lard, and New Forest woodsmen used to cover small cuts with primrose leaves. Juice from the stems rubbed on the face removed unsightly spots, freckles and blemishes.

In Wales primrose juice was a cure for madness

Candied primrose flowers were popular in the seventeenth and eighteenth centuries. When Benjamin Disraeli, Lord Beaconsfield, was dying, Queen Victoria sent him primroses from Balmoral, picked by her own hand. Her note read, 'They were his favourite flower', 'his' meaning Albert, who had died twenty years earlier. Disraeli apparently smiled wanly and said, 'I hope that her Majesty doesn't mean me to deliver them to him in person.' Disraeli had a regular habit of wearing one in his buttonhole, and the Primrose League, founded in his honour in 1883 and disbanded only in 2004, set out to perpetuate his constitutional principles. In 1882 Primrose Day was established on 19 April, and ever since Disraeli's statue in Parliament Square has been decked with primroses. Ironically, primroses are now scarce around Beaconsfield because of over-picking. This is true in many areas of this once widely distributed, insect-pollinated flower, which is the food plant of the Duke of Burgundy butterfly and nine other *Lepidoptera* including the silver-ground carpet and broad-bordered yellow underwing moths.

To John Clare, civilisation was defined by 'a man of taste getting under the tree fullest in leaf to read [a book] & putting in a Primrose between the leaves for a mark & pledge of spring instead of doubling down the leaves—'.

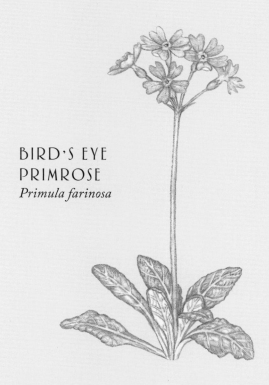

BIRD'S EYE
PRIMROSE
Primula farinosa

POPPY

Papaver species

Thriving on disturbed ground, wild poppies grow in arable fields and wasteland, on roadsides and in meadows. With sedative opiates in the latex, they came to symbolise sleep, and the blood-red petals to represent death. Native to Asia Minor, the bright red field poppy (*P. rhoeas*) probably spread to Western Europe in the seed-corn of early settlers, and images of opium poppies (*P. somniferum*) with their pale mauve (or white, or red) petals have been found in Sumerian artefacts from around 4000BC. The Assyrians called the poppy 'daughter of the fields'.

Poppy seeds were discovered in twelfth-dynasty Egyptian relics dating back 2000 years BC, and evidence shows that the Minoans were acquainted with the making and use of opium. The Romans offered poppies to the dead, especially those they wished to placate.

In the *Georgics*, Virgil directs that the 'Lethean' poppy should be offered as a funeral rite to Orpheus, he who could charm all living things, even the stones, with his music. For the Greeks, the poppy was sacred to Hypnos, god of sleep, great comforter of the world, and symbol of consolation and oblivion. They represented him alongside *Thanatos* (Death) and *Nyx* (Night), crowned with, or holding, poppies.

One poppy stamen alone may produce 2½ million grains of pollen

The red field poppy (*P. rhoeas*) has become an icon of wartime remembrance, ancient symbol of battlefields since at least the twelfth century. In the *Chanson de Roland* Charlemagne, searching for the body of his beloved nephew Roland who died guarding the Pyrenees against *paynims* [pagans] as they advanced through Spain, crossed the meadow at Roncevalles:

> *As the king goes his nephew for to seek*
> *How many flowers he finds upon the lea*
> *Red with the blood of all that chivalry.*

When the battlefield was ploughed after the Duke of Wellington's victory at Waterloo in 1815, carpets of red poppies sprang up. People regarded them as blood spurting from the souls of the slain, and at the 1918 First World War Armistice on 11 November the poppy was adopted as a sign of remembrance. In 2014 the 'Weeping Window' and the 'Wave', centenary commemorations of the outbreak of the Great War, were installed at the Tower of London: 888,246 handmade ceramic red poppies, each representing one British or colonial life lost, were planted until a sea of red poured into the moat, reflecting the words of an unknown soldier who died in Flanders: 'The blood-swept lands and seas of red, where angels fear to tread'.

In mythology the eternal cycle of life and death is inextricably woven with fertility and continuity, and for millennia, more perhaps than any other

wild flower, poppies have been symbols of this cycle. One poppy stamen alone may produce 2½ million grains of pollen (unsurprisingly bees are attracted to poppies), and one plant can produce 17,000 seeds, seeds which can lie dormant for decades, and longer. Thus the ancient Greeks included the poppy in their sacrifices to Demeter, goddess of fertility, whom the Romans named Ceres, goddess of agriculture. The legend goes that, exhausted with grief as she searched for her daughter Proserpina (equivalent to the Greek Persephone) after her rape and abduction to the underworld by Hades god of the underworld, Ceres neglected the land in her charge. Somnus, god of sleep, administered poppy seeds to help her sleep. Body and spirit restored, she returned to her work to help the corn flourish.

> *Here in this tale of trifle let me speak of Ceres' poppy—*
> *Hers it is because, mourning the loss of her stolen daughter,*
> *She is said to have eaten poppy to drown her sorrow, deep*
> *Beyond measure – to forget, as she longed to forget,*
> *Her grief of mind.*

So wrote Walafrid Strabo in his charming *Hortulus* or 'Little Garden', a gem of ninth-century garden literature.

With a history going back some six thousand years it's hardly surprising that there is much folklore about the powers of the poppy. Associated with Aphrodite, it has the property of inspiring love. In Persian literature, red poppies are the eternal lover's flower, a symbol of people who died for love. In country lore, scattering poppy seeds around the bed on St Andrew's night (30 November) would conjure dreams of your future husband. The poppy could also test fidelity: if you place a petal in the left hand and hit it hard with the right, it should snap. If there is no snapping sound, you are insincere (this was practised in Italy and Switzerland even up to the end of the nineteenth century). Sending a dog to retrieve a piece of poppy cake will provide the direction from which true love will appear, and putting a question about love into an empty seed pod under your pillow will provide the answer in a dream. On a more sinister note, hide poppy seeds in a bride's shoe to make her infertile.

Folklore provides a tip should you be pursued by vampires and demons: they have an obsessive compulsion to count poppy seeds, so scattering the seeds in their path will slow them down. Witches grow poppies in their gardens to provide an ingredient of their flying mixtures. Eating a cake made with poppy seeds on New Year's Eve will ensure abundance for the following year. Or, soak poppy seeds in wine for fifteen days and drink for five days while fasting in order to become invisible. Put poppies in your roof timbers and they will ward off lightning – but if you pick poppies you will cause a thunderstorm. In any case the petals droop immediately, prompting some philosophising from Robert Burns:

> Pleasures are like poppies spread
> You seize the flow'r, its bloom is shed.

The bright red of the common poppy is so dazzling that it was believed staring into the centre of the flower would cause temporary blindness. A poppy held near the ear would cause earache: conversely it would cure it. Opium poppy was thought to be the gall which, mixed with vinegar, was offered to Christ on the Cross, and refused by Him. Poppy petals have been used as a colouring agent since the fifteenth century, when it was discovered that steeping the petals in a small amount of hot water and alcohol makes red ink. A poppy is depicted on the back of the Macedonian 500-denar banknote, and is also part of the coat-of-arms of the Republic. Unsurprisingly, opium poppies appear on the royal coat of arms of the Royal College of Anaesthetists.

Poppy seeds are low in opiates but rich in oil, carbohydrate, calcium and protein. The Greeks and Romans mixed them with honey and egg-yolk to eat on bread, and Olympic athletes were prescribed a diet of poppy seeds with honey and wine. Bagels are traditionally sprinkled with poppy seeds, and poppy-seed muffins are universally popular. There's a traditional Middle Eastern cake made with roasted poppy seeds, and in Persian cuisine poppy seeds are sprinkled on to rice dishes. 'Four-flower tea' using poppies, cudweed, mallow and coltsfoot (or a seven-flower tea adding marsh mallow, mullein and violet) helps you sleep. Or you can make a tea with a handful of dried poppy petals to two pints of boiling water, or add the infusion to bath water (or both). An oil from crushed poppy seeds makes a delicious salad-dressing oil, and is used in some margarines.

Opium is extracted from the milky juice of the unripe seed capsules of the opium poppy (*P. somniferum*) and is a dangerous drug. Morphine, heroin, codeine and laudanum derive from it. Widely cultivated, opium poppy production is monitored by international agencies, and is illegal in some countries, but its effects have been known ever since Ancient Egyptian medicine prescribed opium poppy seeds to relieve pain. An opium syrup features in eleventh-century Arab medicine, and *The Grete Herball* of 1526 instructs, 'The quantity of a gram of opium taken in the body mortifieth all the wits of man in such a manner that he feeleth no pain and causeth him to sleep.' It was used for the treatment of gout and St Anthony's fire or ergotism, which is gangrenous poisoning by the wheat fungus ergot, and also known as Holy Fire. Herbalists used it for its analgesic properties, using the fresh petals of field poppy for a syrup to relieve coughs, colds, bronchitis, asthma, mild pain caused by earache, toothache and neuralgia as well as for anxiety and insomnia. But it

WELSH POPPY
Papaver cambricum

PRICKLY POPPY
Papaver argemone

comes with a warning: Marlowe's Jew of Malta 'drank poppy and cold mandrake juice, and being asleep belike they thought me dead, and threw me over the walls'. John Clare obviously knew the effects of 'dropping down' as he called it, to get close up and personal with field poppies and inhale their scent:

> *Corn poppies that in crimson dwell*
> *Call'd headaches from their sickly smell*

From the seventeenth century onwards, opium smoking spread from China to the West. Foreign traders (primarily British) started exporting opium illegally in the eighteenth century and the Opium Wars of the nineteenth century were triggered in 1839 when the Chinese government confiscated and destroyed more than 20,000 chests of opium – about 1,400 tons of the drug – warehoused at Canton by British merchants.

Opium has famously inspired the Muses, but not without side effects. Coleridge was addicted to laudanum, a tincture of opium, describing his habit as 'an insanity ... which none but the Soul's physician can cure'. De Quincey spawned the genre of drug-addiction literature in his *Confessions of an English Opium Eater*, and Berlioz used it to inspire his *Symphonie Fantastique*. Its dangers were, and are, well-known: the poppy's best-known alkaloid, morphine, is extremely toxic, together with its derivative diamorphine, better known as heroin. Since its isolation from opium early in the nineteenth century, morphine became an occasional murder weapon, famously used by convicted murderer Dr Harold Shipman to poison his patients.

The poppy has a myriad of common names: corn-rose, head-ache, blind eyes, sleepy head, ear-aches, poison poppy, ridweed, redweed, thunderbolts, thundercup, thunderflower, corn poppy, pield poppy, Flanders poppy, red poppy, and more. My favourite is the Anglo-Saxon *popig*. *Papaver* is from the Latin word for swelling, referring to the seed capsules, and *rheo* comes either from the Greek verb 'to flow', or from the Latin for 'red'.

LONG-HEADED
POPPY
Papaver dubium

OPIUM
POPPY
Papaver somniferum

213

214

SCARLET PIMPERNEL

Anagallis arvensis

No heart can think, no tongue can tell
The virtues of the pimpernel
TRADITIONAL

Rustic barometers, the orangey-red flowers of scarlet pimpernel open up when the sun shines, and close their petals as skies darken before a storm. So scarlet pimpernel has acquired local names of poor man's weatherglass, shepherd's barometer, poor man's barometer, shepherd's weatherglass and shepherd's clock. Because the flowers close at twilight, and reopen in morning sunshine, they are also known as wink-a-peep and owl's eye – or red chickweed after the plant's sprawling habit as it straggles over the ground, naturalistically illustrated in a sixth-century codex of Dioscorides.

This common weed of arable land and waste places grows in loamy soils, and is mostly annual, although occasionally perennial. It grows worldwide, preferring light shade or full sun. It's a welcome visitor in cottage gardens, where its red stars twinkle among border plants and over rock gardens, flowering from March to May, and then again from August to October. It can be grown in pots from seed, too, and placed on sunny window-sills where it will continue flowering until late in the year.

> **The Irish maintained that carrying a scarlet pimpernel enabled you to understand the language of birdsong**

Famously, the flower gave its name to a novel and play by Baroness Orczy, set during the French Revolution, in which an English aristocrat, a reckless daredevil with the nickname Scarlet Pimpernel, rescues his French counterparts from the guillotine and signs his messages with the drawing of this small red flower.

> *We seek him here, we seek him there,*
> *Those Frenchies seek him everywhere.*
> *Is he in heaven? – Is he in Hell?*
> *That damned elusive Pimpernel.*

Scarlet pimpernel is a magical flower, to such an extent that it was said if you dropped it in water, it would float upstream against the current. Anyone holding it would acquire the gift of second sight, enabling them to communicate with animals and spirits. The Irish maintained that carrying a scarlet pimpernel enabled you to understand the language of birdsong. Some villagers followed a traditional ritual of collecting the flower in silence before sunrise, and bidding it good morning three times before saying anything else: throwing it into the air, it then became an infallible protection. Its powers were noted in an ancient Scandinavian manuscript:

> *Ye man yt beryth it day or nyth*
> *Wekked spryt of hym shal han no myth [power].*

Scarlet pimpernel's curative powers derived from a legend that it first sprang up at Calvary from the fallen drops of Christ's blood. Medieval herbalists claimed therefore that the fresh leaves pressed against the skin could draw out arrows or splinters embedded in the flesh. Pliny recommended it for epilepsy and depression, and the plant was used in melancholia and brain disorders. The ancient Greeks also used it for treating eye disorders, using the juice to dilate the pupils during cataract surgery.

In folk medicine, decoctions of scarlet pimpernel cured eye complaints, hypochondria, toothache, liver and kidney disorders, melancholy, epilepsy, rheumatism, snakebites and the 'bitings of madde dogges'. Pimpernel water eradicates freckles, and Culpeper notes 'the distilled water or juice is much esteemed by French dames to cleanse the skin from any roughnesse'. The plant was used to treat coughs, liver and kidney complaints, and applied externally for joint pain. Scarlet pimpernel is still occasionally prescribed in homeopathy.

Pimpernel water eradicates freckles

A member of the primrose family, pimpernel derives from 'pepper', either from the taste of the leaves which were eaten in the Middle Ages as a culinary herb (although now it is said to be poisonous to humans, dogs and horses if ingested in large quantities, and possibly causes dermatitis if handled), or from the resemblance of its ripe fruits to peppercorns. These seeds remains viable in soil for at least ten years. *Anagallis* come from a Greek word for 'delight', or laughter: *Arvensis*, 'of the fields'.

> *Watch, little field mouse, watch where you tread;*
> *Sparks are falling among the grass,*
> *Think not a flower could burn so red.*
> WALTER MADELY, *THE POOR MAN'S GARDEN*

SELF HEAL

Prunella vulgaris

Wild flower of woodland glades and meadows, self heal grows freely on grassy verges and often appears on unmown lawns. Forming a cylindrical spike on a short stem, the deep imperial-purple flowers have been used in Chinese medicine for liver complaints for two thousand years, with frequent mentions in the medical literature of the Han Dynasty (206BC–AD23).

Known as carpenter's herb, self heal is effective in healing wounds inflicted by chisels, sickles (it is also known as sickle-wood and sicklewort) and other sharp instruments of the woodworker's trade. Some call it hook-weed, after the hooked upper lip of the calyx. Also known as woundwort, self heal was traditionally used to stem the flow of blood from deep cuts. 'The decoction of Prunell [self heal] made with wine or water, doth join together and make whole and sound all wounds, both inward and outward, even as Bugle [*Ajuga reptans*] doth,' wrote John Gerard in his *Herbal* of 1597. 'In the world there are not two better wound herbes, as hath often been proved.' The plant, also called all-heal, touch-and-heal and hearts' ease, was deemed to have such health-giving properties that anyone could cure himself with it without the help of a doctor.

Country people also used self heal as a mouthwash and gargle, and in the sixteenth century believers in the Doctrine of Signatures who saw in the corolla the shape of an open mouth with swollen glands used it to treat diseases of the throat like quinsy and diphtheria. 'Brunelle', whence *Prunella vulgaris* gets its scientific name, comes from the German *breune*, a sore throat, which in turn gave its name to the kind of quinsy or throat abscess self heal was used to treat. The last of the great herbalists, botanist John Parkinson, gave this remedy for mouth ulcers in 1640: 'the juice mixed with a little Hony of Roses, clenseth and healeth all ulcers and sores in the mouth and throate'. Gerard recommended it as a definitive cure for a headache: 'Prunell bruised wit oile of Roses and Vinegar and laied on the forepart of the head, swageth and helpeth the paine and aking thereof.' In present day herbal medicine in the West, its antiviral and antioxidant properties are used against feverish colds and flu, against herpes and against AIDS, and to normalise thyroid function. Medical research is investigating its usefulness against diabetes and high blood pressure.

> *Known as Carpenter's Herb, self heal is effective in healing wounds inflicted by chisels*

SNOWDROP

Galanthus nivalis

An angel flew down to console Eve as she bemoaned the barren soil of Eden after the Fall of Man. Snow was falling, and the angel caught a flake of snow, breathed on it and commanded it to take life. It flowered as soon as it touched the ground. A snowdrop. Eve smiled, realising there was hope, and came to prize it above all others of the flowers in Paradise. The angel flew back up to heaven, and where angel feet had stood, a ring of snowdrops sprang up.

Historians think snowdrops were introduced into Britain by Italian monks in the late fifteenth century: they are not truly native anywhere in Britain, except possibly in Wales, and not recorded as a wild plant until 1583 by the Flemish horticulturalist Charles de L'Écluse. Although they were cultivated in gardens from then on, wild snowdrops weren't mentioned until the 1770s, in Gloucestershire and Worcestershire, and it's probable that these were escapees. Snowdrops have now naturalised widely in damp woods and by streams throughout Britain although not, interestingly, in Ireland.

> *The 'snow-piercer', remains the flower of hope, pushing its way through the snow*

The 'snow-piercer' remains, from the time of St Francis of Assisi in the thirteenth century up to today, the flower of hope. It's one of the first to push its way into the dark days of winter, flowering from January to March. It cuts through the frozen soil like a spear, leaves tightly bound by a small leaf-like spathe sheathing the tip of the flowering stem. For all their apparent delicacy, these winter flowers survive freezing temperatures, possessing anti-freeze proteins that inhibit ice crystals forming and protecting the cells from damage. They may show signs of stress, but because the plant tissue is fundamentally undamaged, the plant recovers as snows thaw and temperatures rise. The white bell-shape emerges, nodding and drooping under three spreading sepals that shelter white, green-tipped petals, providing an early feast for the bees that pollinate it.

In the language of flowers, snowdrops stand for hope, purity, humility, gratitude and virgin innocence. They are often found in churchyards and around monastic ruins, since Candlemas bells were grown in monasteries and convents for those qualities, symbolised by the milk-white, modestly hanging flowers. They are the flower of the Purification of the Virgin Mary, the Feast of Candlemas, which falls on 2 February:

> *The snowdrop, in purest white array*
> *First rears its head on Candlemas Day.*

After Candlemas the image of the Virgin was removed from the altar, and snowdrops, representing purity, were strewn in its place. They are also known as Mary's tapers because when Our Lady went to visit her cousin Elizabeth, snowdrops blossomed where she trod. Candlemas celebrates in parallel the presentation of Jesus at the Temple, and according to legend snowdrops also sprang up in his footsteps.

In folklore, it's unlucky to bring the first – or any single – snowdrop into the house, because it will cause a death: country people associated it with a corpse in a shroud, and they blamed all February deaths on it. It was safer to pick a handful, so some people brought a bunch indoors as protection. But don't pick snowdrops before St Valentine's Day if you want to be married within the year.

Snowdrops are rarely mentioned in the old herbals apart from in a poultice of the crushed bulbs applied externally to frostbite. However, scientists in Eastern Europe have recently extracted galantamine from snowdrops, a substance which appears to stimulate the regeneration of nerve cells, possibly being of benefit in neuralgic disorders and degenerative diseases including Alzheimer's.

The snowdrop – snow bells, fair maid of February, February fairmaids – is not only a drop of snow, it was a snowy drop to wear as an earring or pendant, fashionable in the sixteenth and seventeenth centuries. The original Greek name means 'milkflower of the snow': *gala* is 'milk', *anthos* 'flower', and *nivalis* 'of the snow'.

SPEEDWELL

Veronica species

On the way to Golgotha, place of the skull, a woman stepped forward as Jesus staggered under the weight of the Cross. She wiped His sweating, bleeding forehead pierced by the Crown of Thorns, and an image of His face was imprinted on the woman's handkerchief, a *vera* icon, true image of the Son of God. The botanical genus *Veronica* is named after this apocryphal holy woman, the markings on the petals of speedwell species representing the traces remaining on the cloth.

In the language of flowers, the *Veronicas* represent fidelity. *V. chamaedrys*, or germander speedwell, bright blue wayside flower of spring hedgerows, is the commonest of the species, and 'speeds- you-well', offering protection on a journey. With its meaning of 'prosper well, get well', the flower brought good luck and good health. In

Ireland, travellers had speedwell sewn into their clothes to protect them from accidents. In other places its name was a synonym for 'farewell', since the flowers fall off the stems soon after they are picked.

A member of the Figwort family, with 28 native species and 250 species worldwide, speedwell was an official herb in medieval times. *Veronica officinalis* or heath speedwell was commonly used as a wound-healer, and had a reputation as a healing plant, particularly for skin complaints: 'The water of Veronica distilled with wine, and re-distilled so often until the liquor wax of a reddish colour, prevaileth against the old cough, the dryness of the lungs, and all ulcers and inflammations of the same', writes sixteenth-century herbalist John Gerard. In the eighteenth century people were so convinced that speedwell cured gout that it almost disappeared from around London because of over-picking. *Veronica* was prescribed 'to be taken in the spring for some time, especially by Persons who drink much ale and are in gross habit of body'.

In Ireland, travellers had speedwell sewn into their clothes to protect them from accidents

To gaze closely into a speedwell flower for any length of time is to be dazzled by its intense blue and the startlingly white 'eye' at the centre of the four tiny petals. It sprawls around damp woods and shady places, a perennial with slightly pointed oval leaves. Germander speedwell is a food plant of the heath fritillary butterfly, and two moths including the brown plume. Llewellyn the Great adopted speedwell as his badge when his family held out against the English Kings John, Henry II and Edward I. Anne Pratt, nineteenth-century botanical illustrator, describes 'its brilliant blue blossoms lying like gems among the bright May grasses'. The heavenly blue of *V. chamaedrys* wins for it the Welsh name of eye of Christ. In William Curtis's *Flora Londiniensis* he remarks, 'many plants with less beauty are cultivated in our gardens with the greatest care'.

There are other versions of how the Veronicas came to be so-called: that the name came from the Vettones, a race of ancient Spain; or that it came from two Greek words *phero* (I bear) and *nike* (victory) after its medicinal powers. Speedwell's local names include Billie bright-eye, bright-eye, birds eye, eye of the Child Jesus, farewell, goodbye, cats' eyes, eyebright, wish-me-well, angels' eyes, blue eyes, blue star, God's eye, lark's eye, love-me-not, poor man's tea and wish-me-well.

SPIKED
SPEEDWELL
Veronica spicata

WATER
SPEEDWELL
Veronica anagallis-aquatica

ST JOHN'S WORT

Hypericum perforatum

St John's wort doth charm all the witches away,
If gathered at midnight on the saint's holy day,
And devils and witches have no power to harm
Those that do gather the plant for a charm;
Rub the lintels and post with that red juicy flower
No thunder or tempest will then have the power
To hurt or to hinder your houses; and bind
Round your neck a charm of similar kind.

STAFFORDSHIRE FOLKLORE

226

Herb of St John the Baptist, this major plant of midsummer magic is an obvious sun-symbol with its golden-yellow starburst flowers. Country folk picked St John's wort on the eve of his feast day, 24 June, as a protection against evil spirits – an adaptation of pre-Christian midsummer practices. They gathered them early in the morning while still wet with dew, believing it dangerous to do so after sunrise, and made garlands to hang over the door to protect the house from storms and midsummer ghosts:

> *Trefoil, Vervain, John's Wort, and Dill*
> *Hinder witches from their will.*

As sixteenth-century astrologer Anthony Ascham wrote, 'the virtue of it is thus, if it be put in a man's house, then shal come no wicked spirit therein', and one of St John's wort's ancient names is *fuga daemonium*, or Devil's flight: it was believed that the Devil's hatred of this plant was so great that he tried to destroy it with a needle – or stabbed it frenziedly with a dagger – which is why spots or pricks appear on the leaves on 29 August, the day of John the Baptist's beheading. The red sap in the stems and the red spots issued from the blood of the saint, strengthening the powers of the plant rather than weakening them as the Devil had hoped.

The eve of St John's day was a dangerous time when goblins, witches and ghosts were at large. As darkness fell, people lit midsummer's eve bonfires, throwing St John's wort into the flames to stimulate the sun in its decline. The flower was *sol terrestris*, the sun that disperses darkness, just as St John the Baptist proclaimed the coming of the Light of life to scatter the darkness of death. People leapt through the dwindling flames in a purification ritual, and smoked the leaves over the fire to intensify their exorcising properties, ready for use on St John's day itself.

If a young girl picked a flower of St John's wort with dew on it, she would marry within the year, and if she placed it on her pillow and it was still fresh the next morning, her chances were similar. If a childless woman walked naked to pick St John's wort she would conceive within the year, and with a sprig tied to the cradle no child could be taken for a changeling. If a woman believed herself possessed, she placed leaves from St John's wort on her bosom and strewed them around the house. But it was dangerous to step on St John's wort, since a fairy horse would whisk you away to a distant place and then vanish, leaving you stranded. In France they call Midsummer's Eve *chasse diable*, and St John's wort *tout sain*, all holy, so powerful was it. *Avoir toutes les herbes de St Jean* means to be ready for anything – and such were the plant's properties that King George VI named one of his racehorses Hypericum.

> *It was believed that the Devil's hatred of this plant was so great that he tried to destroy it with a needle*

The most powerful plant in our flora against evil, St John's wort is an effective medicine too. A wound herb praised from Dioscorides to Culpeper, it's an infallible balm when soaked in oil and applied to lesions. St John's wort salve continues to be made and marketed for healing burns and sunburn, for bed sores or nerve pain, since its active ingredient hypericin is a natural antibiotic as well as being anti-inflammatory. It has anti-depressant properties too, and is marketed as an effective remedy for clinical depression. This was long recognised in folk medicine over the centuries, widely used in 'melancholy' and 'nervous disorders'. It is a sedative, and enough of a painkiller to treat headaches and rheumatism. The red oil prepared by macerating the herb in olive oil is still used for chest complaints, and as a poultice for sprains. St John's wort is used in modern herbal medicine as a cure for neuritis and the prevention of haemorrhaging.

But principally the red perforations and spots on the leaves, signifying the pores of the skin, relate it to skin traumas and especially to open wounds. Commemorated as Balm of the Warrior's Wound, St John's wort was so important to the Knights of St John as a treatment in the Crusades that they got their ladies at home to treat their wounds with it on their return. Gerard insisted 'In time of wars no gentelwoman should be without St John's wort', and that it was 'a most pretious remedie for deep wounds and those that are thorow the body'. St John's wort is still an emblematic flower of the St John Ambulance Brigade.

There are numerous species of St John's wort growing in grassy places and hedgerows, evergreen and perennial with masses of cheerful yellow flowers, which attract moths. The flowers vary in size, with bushy stamens, and appear from July to September. With its large flowers, Rose of Sharon (*H. calycinum*) is one of the best known, introduced from Turkey in the seventeenth century and now used widely in urban planting. Tutsan (*H. androsaemum*), often seen in woodland and hill country, gets its name either from *tout sain*, all holy (as the herb of St John) or *toute saine*, all healthy (after its medicinal properties). If St John's wort was found growing in pasture land, it was thought the herd's prosperity was ensured – although ingesting the plant may cause redness and itching of skin, and turn the milk pinkish. The tops of the young plants, when mordanted with alum, give a yellowish-red dye once used in Scottish tartans.

There are two versions of how the plant got its generic name *Hypericum*: either from Greek words meaning 'under' and 'hedge', where it often flourishes (the yew along my cottage boundary is underplanted with a bank of *Hypericum*, and is a delight throughout the year), or 'over' and 'icon', alluding to its supernatural powers. The specific *perforatum* is because the leaves appear perforated with tiny punctures. William Turner was the first to name it in 1538, calling it St Johannes Gyrs (grass), from the medieval name *Herba Sancta Joannis*. In 1551 he renamed it St John's Wort. Local names include Mary's glory (Ireland), grace of God, John's grass, Bethlehem star, St Peterwort and rosin rose.

230

THISTLES

Carduus, Cirsium and Onopordum species

Cut dashels [thistles] in June – it's a month too soon
Cut in July – they're sure to die.
TRADITIONAL

There are fourteen species of thistle native to Great Britain, of a huge plant family with as many practical uses as its copious history and folklore. Shakespeare conflates 'rough Thistles' with 'hateful Docks', and biblically thistles represent sin and disgrace because where God cursed the ground in Eden, it brought forth thistles and thorns.

Yet thistles have proved useful to the human race in ways weird and wonderful. Pliny states, and medieval writers repeat, that a decoction of thistles applied to a bald head would restore a healthy growth of hair. Gerard tells us on the authority of Dioscorides and Pliny that 'the leaves and root thereof are a remedy for those that have their bodies drawn backwards', and Culpeper explains that not only is the juice therefore good for a crick in the neck, but that it's a remedy for rickets in children. Some considered thistles to bring good fortune, to be a protection against evil and to bestow strength and energy. If you put a thistle flower in your pocket it would ward off evil and melancholy, and grown in the garden it would deter thieves from your house. And wizards made the tallest ones into wands.

But there's more to thistles than whimsy. The seeds of many species yield a good oil by expression, and have been used for burning, to light lamps and for culinary purposes (1lb of the seeds produce, expressed with heat, about 1 pint of oil). The down of musk thistle (*Carduus nutans*) has been used in paper-making, and that of the

231

cotton thistle (*Onopordum acanthium*) was collected from the stem and used to stuff pillows. Some thistles are grown for their ornamental value: the *Echinops* genus contains more than a hundred species of globe thistles, particularly prized for their showy flowers. The generic name is a clue to another use: the greater number of thistles are assigned to the genus *Carduus*, a name of uncertain derivation which may come from the Greek *cheuro*, a technical word for carding wool, for which thistle heads have been used.

Pliny states, and medieval writers repeat, that a decoction of thistles applied to a bald head would restore a healthy growth of hair

In the past, heads of thistles were boiled, and the young stems stripped of their rind to be eaten, dipped in melted butter like asparagus. Thistle leaves have provided excellent food for cattle and horses, beaten up or crushed in a mill to destroy the prickles – widely used in Scotland before the introduction of special fodder crops. Europeans also ate milk thistle leaves in salad, or as a spinach substitute. The flowers can be steamed and eaten like artichokes, and of course the well-known globe artichoke, a non-native species believed to come from the Mediterranean and Canary Islands, is a common edible thistle.

Thistles are one of our oldest ornamental and heraldic devices, particularly associated with Scottish history. On an altarpiece in Holyrood Palace painted around 1485 during the reign of James III, thistles appear on the tapestry depicted behind the kneeling figure of Queen Margaret. By 1503 the flower had become the national badge. The thistle appears on gold coins of 1525 and on silver groats showing James V, and occupies the centre of James VI's coinage. It appears on James VI's great Seal of 1583, and after his accession to the English throne in 1601 the thistle was united with the rose. Ironically, the

Scotch or cotton thistle (*Onopordum acanthium*) is relatively rare in Scotland and was introduced by the Romans as an ornamental plant into England, probably to East Anglia.

The Order of the Thistle. the most ancient of British Orders, with the exception of the Order of the Garter, was instituted in 1540 by James V of Scotland. The Order consists of the Sovereign and sixteen knights and ladies, as well as certain 'extra' knights who include members of the British Royal Family and foreign monarchs. The Sovereign alone grants membership of the Order, and is not advised by the Government as with other orders. The Order's primary emblem is the thistle, national flower of Scotland, and the motto is *Nemo me impune lacessit*, 'No one attacks me with impunity', rendered in Scots as 'Wha daur meddle wi' me?'

The blessed thistle, *Carduus* or *Cnicus benedictus*, also known as Holy Thistle, has a reputation as a heal-all. It was mentioned in all the treatises on the plague as a specific remedy, as expounded in the *Poore Man's Jewell, that is to say, a Treatise of the Pestilence, unto which is annexed a declaration of the vertues of the Hearbes Carduus Benedictus and Angelica*, published by Thomas Brasbridge in 1578: 'The distilled leaves helpeth the hart, expelleth all poyson taken in at the mouth and other corruption that doth hurt and annoye the hart, and the juice of it is outwardly applied to the bodie'. Gerard recommends the leaves 'for stubburne and rebellious ulcers', and they were a never-failing cure for any wound or sore. They destroyed worms, and when taken in a warm infusion cured fevers, bad colds and headaches. Since then, research has shown that the plant contains cnicin, a lactone with properties analogous to salicin from which aspirin is derived. Shakespeare advises in *Much Ado about Nothing*, 'get you some of this distilled *Carduus benedictus*, and lay it to your heart: it is the only thing for a qualm ... I mean plain Holy Thistle'.

The Blessed Thistle is native to Southern Europe, growing readily in England where it has been cultivated for several centuries for its medicinal uses, although milk thistle, *Silybum marianum*, also known

WELTED
THISTLE
Carduus acanthoides

SPEAR
THISTLE
Cirsium vulgare

MARSH
THISTLE
Cirsium palustre

SLENDER THISTLE
Carduus tenuiflorus

MELANCHOLY THISTLE
Cirsium heterophyllum

COTTON OR SCOTCH THISTLE
Onopordum acanthium

as Marian thistle, is the most important medicinally among the members of the genus. The ancients used it for cancerous complaints, and in medieval Europe it was a remedy for snakebite and rabies. In more modern times the juice was applied to canker sores and ulcers. It is said to improve the purification and circulation of the blood, and to strengthen the brain and the memory. In some districts the leaves are called pig leaves, because pigs like them. The seeds of the milk thistle are a favourite food of goldfinches, whereas butterflies flock to the welted (*Carduus acanthoides*) and creeping (*Cirsium arvense*) thistles, the former being the food plant of the painted lady, the latter host to the thistle gall fly.

The seeds of milk thistle were often used in medicinal preparations for conditions of the gallbladder and liver, including hepatitis and cirrhosis. William Westmacott, author of *A Scripture Herbal*, writes of this thistle in 1694: 'It is a Friend to the Liver and Blood: the prickles cut off, they were formerly used to be boiled in the Spring and eaten with other herbs; but as the World decays, so doth the Use of good old things and others more delicate and less virtuous brought in.' It has been used as a remedy for liver complaints for two thousand years, its properties protecting liver cells from toxins, and helping cells regenerate. It has proved helpful for a hangover or simple indigestion. You can use milk thistle products before drinking alcohol to limit its effects and protect against potential damage.

Milk thistle was included in Renaissance herbal collections, where it was listed as useful to 'expel melancholie' (Gerard 1597), as a 'friend to the liver and bloode' (Westmacott 1694), as good for obstructions of the liver and spleen, for jaundice, and for kidney stones (Culpeper 1653). There's a tradition that the white veins of the leaves came from the milk of the Virgin Mary, which once fell on them, hence a local name of Our Lady's thistle. Because the veins contain a white liquid, the plant was considered useful for stimulating lactation, and this is the use to which it is chiefly put. A warm infusion is recommended for nursing mothers to procure a good supply of milk. It scarcely ever fails to procure a good supply of breast milk, and is one of the best medicines for the purpose.

The Carline thistle's name was originally 'Carolina', after the eighth-century Frankish emperor Charlemagne (Carolus Magnus), according to this contemporary chronicler: 'a horrible pestilence broke out in his army and carried off many thousand men, which greatly troubled the pious emperor. Wherefore he prayed earnestly to God, and in his sleep there appeared to him an angel who shot an arrow from a crossbow, telling him to mark the plant upon which it fell, for with that plant he might cure his army of the pestilence.' Carline thistle has camphor-like properties, which are antiseptic. In Anglo-Saxon times it was called ever-throat meaning 'boar's throat', from the bristly appearance of the flowerheads, and used as a charm against bad luck and ill-health.

The root of dwarf thistle, *Carduus acaulis*, was at one time chewed as a remedy for toothache, and decoction of the root diminished discharge from mucous membranes. It was thought also to be good in nervous complaints. Melancholy thistle, *Carduus heterophyllum*, is said to have been the original badge of the House of Stuart, not the cotton thistle. It is more common in Scotland than in England, and Culpeper considered that a decoction of this thistle in wine 'being drank expels melancholy from the body and makes a man as merry as a cricket'. He is spicing up two-thousand-year-old wisdom here: 'Dioscorides saith, the root borne about one doth the like, and removes al diseases of melancholy: modern writers laugh at him: let them laugh that win: my opinion is, that it is the best remedy against all melancholy diseases that grows: they that please may use it.'

Thistles are a butterfly plant: the black-veined white nectars on spear thistle, the white-letter hairstreak on creeping thistle, and the painted lady on several species. In the language of flowers the thistle stands for nobility and, unlikely as it may seem, the generic *Carduus* may possibly be the derivation of the name of a certain village in Saône-et-Loire world-famous for its wine: Chardonnay.

238

VERVAIN

Verbena officinalis

It seems incongruous that such an insignificant-looking plant should have played so significant a role in western cultural imagination, but from Mesopotamia to Ancient Greece and Rome vervain was 'the enchanter's plant', one with highly sacred and magic properties. Even today in France it's known as *herbe sacrée*. A plant of purification, the Greeks brushed clean the festival table of Zeus with vervain, their 'holy herb'. before special occasions. They intertwined Aphrodite's crown of myrtle with vervain, and dedicated it to the goddess of beauty. Its mystical powers came to be connected with love charms, and well into medieval times vervain was used in charms and love-philtres. According to the Greeks, it was an aphrodisiac with the power of reviving lost love, and would reconcile enemies. Conversely, in Laurence Sterne's *Tristram Shandy*, when Uncle Toby is due to court the widow Wadman at close quarters, he is advised to moderate his passions with an infusion of vervain.

> *The Greeks brushed clean the festival table of Zeus with vervain, their 'holy herb', before special occasions*

To the Romans, vervain was an herb of good omen, Apuleius remarking in the second century that it drove away all poisons. Vervain was the Romans' altar plant, *herba sancta*, and they held an annual festival called *Verbanalia*. They used vervain in religious ceremonies, and its botanical name *Verbena* derives from Latin meaning 'the branches of plants' – the other sacred verbenae being laurel, olive, tamarisk, myrtle and cypress. Virgil, in the twelfth book of the *Aeneid*, suggests that vervain has supernatural powers, and that before battle certain men were 'clad in priestly dress and had their brows bound with vervain'. It afforded protection, according to an anonymous text: 'If one goes into battle, let him seek the vervain and keep it in his clothes and he will escape from his enemies. They that bear vervain upon them shall have love and grace of great masters.' Roman heralds, messengers and ambassadors wore it as a badge of office.

Standing for enchantment in flower language, this extremely magical and powerful plant was used by witches in their spells, although this could work both ways, protecting people from witches:

> *Vervain and Dill*
> *Hinder witches from their will.*

Vervain was one of the plants hung over the door on St John's Eve, 23 June, to defend the house against evil spirits: 'Bring your garlands,' advised Ben Johnson, 'and with reverence place vervain upon the altar.' The anonymous tract *Ye Popish Kingdom* of the sixteenth century records how:

> *'Young men round about with maides doe dance in every streete*
> *With garlands wrought of Motherwort, or else with vervaine sweete'*

A symbol of enchantment 'agaynst witchcraft much avayling', vervain was doubly potent, being for white magic and against black magic. From ancient times the plant was used in sacrificial rites, and in the Middle Ages the Welsh called it Devil's bane: folk cut it at nightfall, brought it into a darkened church, dipped it into holy water and sprinkled it around. Similarly, it was used in incense for exorcisms.

If you carried vervain it would protect you from the wiles of Satan, or (consequence or contradiction?) bestow eternal youth. Vervain had the power to open locks, and magicians rubbed it all over the body, claiming it enabled you to have your heart's desire. Gerard was sceptical: 'The devil did reveal it as a secret divine medicine,' he declared, going on to say that he would have none of any of this enchantment nonsense: 'many odde old wives' fables are written of vervaine tending to witchcraft and sorcerie, which you may read elsewhere, for I am not willing to trouble your eares with reporting such trifles as honest eares abhorre to heare'. Equally cynical, Robert Turner wrote in 1687, 'It is said to be used by witches to do mischief, and so may all other herbs if by wicked astrologers used to accomplish their wretched ends.'

> *Magicians rubbed it all over the body, claiming it enabled you to have your heart's desire.*

In Britain the Druids held vervain in special reverence: they venerated the plant and offered sacrifices to the earth before ceremoniously cutting it. They decreed that, while chanting secret incantations, vervain 'be gathered about the rising of the dog-star, but so as neither sun nor moon be at that time above the earth to see it'. Druidesses were not allowed to touch it. Anyone who uprooted vervain was expected to put in its place a honeycomb, to make amends for depriving the earth of such a holy herb.

Vervain attracts doves to the dovecote, and in the house, garden or vineyard it attracts wealth. If you feel a touch paranoid, put a baked toad into a silk bag with vervain and hang it around your neck, and evil cannot touch you. Or, simply wearing vervain around your neck will protect you from lightning, nightmares and about thirty ailments.

A remedy going as back as far as Dioscorides in the first century AD persisted: in a 1660 *Book of Notable Things* the author Thomas Lupton says 'the root of vervain hanged at the neck of such as have the King's Evil, it brings a marvellous and unhoped help'. This condition was scrofula, tuberculosis of the lymph glands in the neck,

241

supposed to be curable by the touch of royalty, a custom first adopted in England by Edward the Confessor. As late as 1837, the *London Pharmacopoeia* states that a necklace of vervain roots tied with a yard of white satin would cure you of the King's Evil.

Pliny wrote, 'if the dining chamber be sprinkled with water in which the herb has been steeped for several hours, the guests will become merry and filled with a sense of well-being': worth a try today at a dinner party, since it was a practice that survived for more than a thousand years. It's found in *The Grete Herball* of 1526 (a translation from the French work known as *Le Grant Herbier*): 'To make folke mery at ye table. To make all them in a hous to be mery take foure leaves and fore rotes of vervayne in wyne, than sprynkle the wyne all about the hous where the eatynge is and they shall all be mery.'

> And thou, light vervain, too, thou must go after,
> Provoking easy souls to mirth and laughter.

Christianity absorbed the healing attributes of vervain, which became Herb of the Cross, said to grow at the scene of the Crucifixion and to have staunched Christ's wounds. A seventeenth-century poet, John White, wrote in 1624:

> Hallow'd be thou, Vervain, as thou growest in the ground,
> For in the Mount of Calvary thou first wast found.
> Thou healest our Saviour Jesus Christ
> And staunchest His bleeding wound.

Known as simpler's joy, and found to be antispasmodic, tonic and astringent, vervain has had many uses in folk medicine, not surprisingly for all its magical, mystical and religious virtues. The Hippocratic 400 simples, which separated magic from medicine, used vervain specifically for healing wounds and for nervous disorders. Used in remedies for wounds, stones, gripes, malaria, headaches, sore throats, cancer, eye problems, piles and childbirth (and even the plague), vervain became an official drug used in chronic skin complaints, and to staunch wounds. It has been used in homeopathy to treat epilepsy,

> *And thou, light*
> *vervain, too, thou*
> *must go after,*
> *Provoking easy souls*
> *to mirth and laughter*

asthma, whooping cough and pneumonia. It was also effective – still is – for depression:

> *Black melancholy, rusts, that fed despair*
> *Through wounds' long rage, with sprinkled vervain clear,*

writes the seventeenth-century poet Sir William Davenant. Local names include holy herb, tears of Juno, blood of Mercury, pigeon's grass, and columbine, from the Greek for dove, symbol of the Holy Spirit, because doves were said to like hovering around the plant, as Gerard observed, 'because Pigeons are delighted to be amongst it, as also to eate thereof'.

VIOLET

Viola species

I know a bank whereon the wild thyme blows,
Where oxlips and the nodding violet grows ...
SHAKESPEARE, *A MIDSUMMER NIGHT'S DREAM*

S hining darkly from heart-shaped leaves of deep green, violets
herald spring as the world awakens from winter. These wild
flowers of woodland and wayside have an ability to dazzle as
they peep out of the cold grass, among the first of our wild flowers to
appear. As Shelley wrote,

After the slumber of the year
The woodland violets re-appear.

The *Viola* family is a genus of hundreds of species worldwide. Vigorous spreaders along woodland edges, in clearings and ancient hedgerows, they are often found near monastic ruins, or in cottage gardens. *Viola odorata*, or sweet violet, is the only scented one. Deep purple or white, it's known as wood violet, common violet and English violet. *V. riviniana*, called dog violet because it's inferior to *V.odorata*, being scentless, is lilac, with a darker spur. *V. canina*, the heath–dog violet, has clear bluish flowers with a yellow spur. These, along with *V. hirta*, the hairy violet, *V. palustris*, the marsh violet, and *V. reichenbachiana*, the early dog violet, are the commonest of Britain's wild violets.

From March onwards, flowering too early for bee pollination, violets are cleistogamous (self-fertilising) and they also reproduce through root runners. Grown in pots since earliest times, they were cultivated in medieval and Elizabethan knot gardens, and used as strewing herbs. Their name derives from *vias*, meaning 'wayside', a favourite habitat. Scentless violets have acquired local names of blue mice, pigs violet, and shoes and stockings. They were sometimes known by cuckoo names, too, the cuckoo being harbinger of spring: cuckoo's shoe, cuckoo's stockings and cuckoo's heel, from the spur at the back of the flower.

> *I know a bank whereon the wild thyme blows, Where oxlips and the nodding violet grows...*

Violets are a valuable umbrella species, and play an important role in the ecological chain since their habitats shelter a range of other creatures: spiders, lizards, hazel dormice, scrub warblers and many species of butterfly among them. Violets are the food plant of fritillary butterfly larvae, the dark green, the high brown, the pearl-bordered and the silver-washed fritillaries all laying their eggs on tree trunks close to dog violets. These beautiful butterflies are in decline both in range and abundance, due to the loss of open sunny habitats that violets love. Intensive farming practices, chemical sprays and a decline in woodland management have all played their part.

Such a lovely flower couldn't fail to acquire legendary status. To the Greeks, the violet was a beautiful nymph transformed by the jealous goddess Diana into a flower so that

> *The flower came to represent humility, not just Adam's but Christ's as well, and also became an emblem of constancy*

Apollo would stop chasing after her. Alternatively, when Zeus metamorphosed his lover Io into a white heifer to escape the wrath of Juno, he made sweet violets grow in her meadow. The naming of the chemical constituents of the flower, the ionones, are derived from this myth, added to which the Greek for 'violet' is *ion*, after a legend that some nymphs presented violets to King Ion who had led an Ionian colony into Attica. Yet another story goes that where Orpheus dropped his lute, violets sprang up, but Persephone hated them because it was violets she was gathering when she was snatched back into the underworld by Hades.

Aristophanes described Athens as 'violet-crowned'. The demand for the flowers was so great that violet nurseries abounded. Violet chaplets and garlands were sold in the marketplace in Athens all year round, and frequently offered as gifts. They were thought by some Athenians to moderate anger, procure sleep, and to comfort and strengthen the heart. When a son was born into the family, a garland of violets and roses was hung on the door, and in some places it was a custom to hang a violet garland on your beloved's door. On a certain day in spring all children over the age of three (game survivors in days of high infant mortality) wore a crown of violets.

Christian legends sprang up too: where tears of repentance shed by Adam fell on the ground in the Garden of Eden, violets bloomed. The flower came to represent humility, not just Adam's but Christ's as well, and also became an emblem of constancy, standing for steadfastness in flower language:

> Violet is for faithfulnesse
> Which in me shall abide;
> Hoping likewise that from your heart
> You will not let it slide.

Growing out of season in late summer, violets portend trouble or even death, and are also referred to as a funeral flower. Laertes mourns Ophelia in *Hamlet*:

> Lay her i' the earth;
> And from her fair and unpolluted flesh
> May violets spring.

This is just one of 18 times Shakespeare mentions violets in his works: on one occasion he reminds us of the ephemeral nature of its scent, when Laertes says to Hamlet,

> A violet in the youth of primy nature,
> Forward, not permanent, sweet, not lasting,
> The perfume and supplicance of a minute;
> No more.

And he was right – almost: a major component of the scent of *Viola odorata* is the ketone ionone, which temporarily desensitises olfactory nerve receptors, dulling the sense of smell. It is even on record that gardeners who grow violets in quantity can't smell them after repeated exposure to the scent. The most powerful perfume is found in the

Parma cultivars, grown in the largest commercial plantations near Nice. Their fragrance has been used since earliest times in cosmetic perfumes, and because of the heavy seductive scent the Greeks dedicated the violet to Aphrodite, goddess of love, and her son Priapos. *Priapeion* is one of their names for the flower, and as a symbol of fertility violets appear in the Unicorn Tapestries woven in Flanders around 1500.

The Greeks and Romans drank violet wine, and they made conserves, syrups and confectionery from violets. Crystallised violet petals have decorated desserts for centuries. Rich in vitamins A and C, they have been used in confectionery, made into cordials and put into salads. Violet vinegar has a lovely colour and fragrance and violet leaves are edible too: they contain soothing mucilage and are antibacterial. For two thousand years the flowers have been cultivated as a colouring agent for drinks and syrups, and for the liqueur 'Parfait Amour'. The French make a laxative syrup from violets, although nowadays they use a synthesised extract of violet since an unsustainable number of fresh flowers are required to obtain the oil.

A Gaelic recipe goes, 'Anoint thy face with goats' milk in which violets have been infused, and there is not a young prince on earth who will not be charmed by thy beauty.' Violets have been used in medicine, too: Pliny recommended a liniment of violet root and vinegar for gout and disorders of the spleen. A chaplet of violets on the head would disperse the effects of wine, preventing headaches and dizziness. Applying the leaves was a remedy for bruises, and antiseptic too. Salicylic acid has been obtained from violets, which goes to show the veracity of country wisdom before the days of aspirin: the sixteenth-century herbalist Ascham wrote, 'for thee that may not slepe for sickness seeth this herbe in water and at even let him soke well hys feete in the water to the ancles, wha he goeth to bed, bind of this herbe to his temples'.

The dried leaves and flowers are emetic, hypotensive and diuretic. The leaves are antiseptic, and a plaster of violet leaves was used to cure a mouth ulcer. Gerard's *Herbal* of 1597 goes further: 'The flowers are good for inflammations, especially of the sides and lungs; they take away the hoarsenesse of the chest, the ruggednesse of the winde-pipe and jawes, and take away thirst.' You can make an effective cough mixture with the flowers since they are also expectorant.

Pliny considered that wearing a garland of violets around the head would stop headaches and dizziness, and violets were grown in medieval physic gardens for insomnia. If you get mugged or beaten up, try Richard Surflet's advice in *The Countrie Farme* of 1600: 'He that shall have taken a blow upon the head, so that it hath astonished him, shall not have anie greater hurt, if presently after such a blow he drinke Violet flowrs stampt, and continue the same drinke for a certaine time.'

At the turn of the twentieth century an old wives' tale current in Oxfordshire, that an infusion of 20 violet leaves infused in boiling water would allay cancer pains, was put to the test. In 1902 the sister of the Earl of Romney, Lady Margaret Marsham of Maidstone, had a tumour on one of her tonsils. She started drinking infusions of violet, and made public a remedy for the external swelling: 'A pint of boiling water poured over a handful of violet leaves, allowed to stand 12 hours. Strain and warm a sufficient quantity to be soaked up by a piece of lint. Apply to the affected part and cover with oiled silk. Change the lint when dry or cold.' Within a week, her swelling had disappeared, and she was completely cured.

Napoleon planted Josephine's grave with violets, her favourite flower. One was found in a locket he was wearing on his deathbed, and violets were heaped on the tomb of his great-nephew Napoleon

> *'Anoint thy face with goats' milk in which violets have been infused, and there is not a young prince on earth who will not be charmed by thy beauty.'*

249

III. When Napoleon himself was exiled from France he swore he would return with the violets in the spring, and the violet became the Napoleonic emblem. His supporters toasted him as 'Caporal Violette', and wore violet rings and ribbons. They had a code question, *'Aimez-vous la violette?'* The reply was *'Eh bien, elle reparaîtra en printemps.'* Napoleon was as good as his word: he entered the Tuileries on 20 March, in the violet season.

Queen Victoria loved violets as much as she did primroses: her ladies-in-waiting, and Victorian ladies in high society, had posies made for both day and evening wear. During the Queen's later years, over four thousand violet plants were grown in frames at Windsor to guarantee a constant supply at court. Their significance lingered into the twentieth century, when badges depicting dog violets were sold in fund-raising efforts in the UK and Australia to commemorate soldiers fallen in the First World War.

The violet has spawned many a literary anecdote: John Clare pours scorn on a pretentious poet, one of many city 'literati' of the time who had little familiarity with nature and adored the idea that its sole purpose was to put up a mirror to their narcissistic reflections. Quoting 'My heart is like the violet robbed of breath', Clare retorts 'whoever suspected that the violet had so much breath to part with?' Clare would have enjoyed hearing the poet Walter Landor, whose character is described as 'rumbustious and lively', throwing his cook out of the window in a fit of anger and gazing down at the spot where the man lay, exclaiming, 'Good God! I forgot the violets!'

The sixth-century poet Fortunatus, on sending violets to St Rhadegund, wrote 'Of all the fragrant herbs, none I send can compare with the nobleness of the purple violets; they shine in royal purple, and perfume and beauty unite in their petals. May you show forth in your life the peace they represent.'

YELLOW WOOD
VIOLET
Viola biflora

HEATH-DOG
VIOLET
Viola canina

251

WILD ROSE

Rosa species

In AD850 a rose was planted in Hildesheim in Germany by Charlemagne's son, and it is still blooming today. The 'thousand-year-old rose bush', the world's longest living rose, flourishes over the Romanesque apse of St Mary's cathedral, built in the ninth century at the same time as the rose was planted. Its stem is now a foot thick, the root system buried in the crypt below the choir.

Roses are a massive presence in cultural and natural history. They play a leading role in the collective imagination, with legends concerning their origins in all major religions. Fossil evidence of the species goes back thirty-five thousand years, and four thousand years ago roses were pictured on frescoes in the Minoan palace at Knossos in Crete. They appear in the *Iliad* in the seventh or eighth century BC, with Aphrodite healing Hector's wounds with oil of roses.

The rose became the flower of love for the Greeks, dedicated to Aurora, rosy-fingered goddess of dawn, and roses flourished in ancient Athens in gardens and in nurseries. Continuing into the Roman Empire, it was reported that Cleopatra, at vast expense, arranged for a carpet of rose petals to greet Mark Antony, and at a single festival Nero expended unbalanced amounts of money on roses alone.

It was reported that Cleopatra, at vast expense, arranged for a carpet of rose petals to greet Mark Antony

The rose moved through pagan folklore from Aphrodite to Eros and ultimately morphed into the medieval Rosa Mystica of the Virgin Mary as a symbol of virginity. There's a story that the first roses were white, but some turned red when stained by the blood of, variously, Adonis when wounded by a wild boar, or Aphrodite's foot pierced by a briar when she rushed to help him, or Christ when drops fell from His wounds on the Cross. Furthermore, there's a legend that the Crown of Thorns was made of briars, and where sacred blood fell to the ground, roses sprang up and blossomed:

> *Men saw the thorns on Jesus' brow*
> *But angels saw the roses.*

Like some other shrubs, the wild rose is reputed to have been the burning bush where God appeared to Moses, and also the thicket in which Abraham caught the ram he sacrificed in place of his son Isaac.

Several varieties of wild roses flower in England's hedgerows during June and July, with blossoms from pure white to deep pink. John Clare, in one of his 'Natural History Letters', wrote under 'Wild rose ... there are 3 different sorts about us & a small one that grows in woods has a pleasant smell in its young shoots a sort of bastard sweetbrier—the sweetbrier also grows wild in plenty about our heaths ...' The 'bastard' he mentions is R. *micrantha*, a species similar to *Rosa rubiginosa* (syn. *R. eglanteria*) or sweet briar, from the scent released by the leaves through minuscule glands when pressed. This was the rose Shakespeare called 'eglantine'. Two English poets consider the bright foliage of the wild rose

The rose gives its name to the rosary, prayer beads originally made of rose petals pressed tightly into moulds

worth praising too: Shelley has 'The fresh green leaves of the hedge-row briar', and John Clare on the leaves of the dog rose, 'a glossy green leaf with out hairs & is common in every old hedge'.

The rose gives its name to the rosary, prayer beads originally made of rose petals pressed tightly into moulds, with large beads for the *Pater Noster* and *Credo*, smaller ones for the Ave Maria. The name 'rosary' was coined by St Dominic in 1208 when he introduced the Devotion of the Blessed Virgin Mary to commemorate a vision he had of the Virgin, since when praying the rosary has remained a devotional practice.

The Order of the Golden Rose, the Rosa d'Oro, is conferred by the Pope on chosen people for their devotion to the church. They are presented with a rose tree made by goldsmiths in pure gold, about 30–45cm (12–18in) high. The Blessing of the Golden Rose takes place on the fourth Sunday in Lent, *Dies Domenica in Rosa*, when during a candlelit mass the Pope pours balsam and musk into the heart of the principal rose. Nowadays the Golden Rose is seldom awarded to individuals, although Pope Benedict XVI awarded it to several places of sacred significance during his pontificate.

The red rose was the symbol of the House of Lancaster during the fifteenth-century Wars of the Roses; the white rose the symbol of the House of York. The Greeks dedicated the latter to Harpocrates, god of silence, usually portrayed as a young lad with a finger to his lips. The story goes that Cupid gave him a white rose as a bribe to prevent him from betraying the amorous indiscretions of his mother Venus. The flower was adopted as an emblem of silence, often sculpted into ceilings of drinking and feasting rooms as a warning to guests that what was said under the influence of conviviality should not be repeated. The saying 'under the rose', *sub rosa*, became a synonym for secrecy, and it was in Germany that a rose was first painted or carved on the ceilings of Council Chambers, denoting privacy. King William III communicated to two burgomasters of Amsterdam his scheme to invade England beneath a stucco rose, and a five-petalled rose is sometimes carved on to confessionals of the Catholic Church as a sign of confidentiality.

Pliny called Britain 'Albion' because it was covered with pale wild roses

Red roses in particular are symbols of love almost everywhere in the world, and used in love charms and divination. 'My love is like a red red rose/That's newly sprung in June' is one of Robert Burns's most quoted lines. The rose in flower language is an emblem of passion, and red rose petals were traditionally sewn into muslin bags as a love token. Not entirely unrelated perhaps, the wild rose is an emblem of frailty and mortality, because its flowers live for such a short time. It also, with its contrast of sharp thorns and beautiful, scented flowers, stands for true love that survives both good times and bad: 'Roses have thorns and silver fountains mud', as Shakespeare puts it. Similarly Robert Herrick:

> *Before man's fall the rose was born*
> *St Ambrose says, without the thorn;*
> *But for man's fault then was the thorn*
> *Without the fragrant rose-bud born;*
> *But ne'er the rose without the thorn.*

Rose oil is widely used in perfumery, although wild roses are only faintly scented and are not used commercially in aromatics (R. *damascena* and R. *centifolia* are the principal species cultivated commercially for rose oil). The rose features commonly in heraldry, in coats of arms and in heraldic badges, with five petals, ray-like stamens, and five short pointed leaves beneath. Symbol of the Tudor dynasty, the rose is also much used in regimental colours. On the badge of the UK, the Tudor rose, which combines the white with the red, the Houses of York and Lancaster, stands between thistle (for Scotland) and shamrock (for Ireland) issuant from the same stalk.

To dream of being pricked by a briar as you try to pick a rose through the branches means you are in love. Young girls in Somerset used to perform a Midsummer's Eve ritual at the stroke of midnight, reciting:

> *Rose leaves, rose leaves*
> *Rose leaves I strew*
> *He that will love me*
> *Come after me now.*

Turning, the girls would see an apparition of their lover behind them. To dream of roses foretells success in love, particularly if the roses are red. If a single girl dreams of picking them it means she will fall in love with a handsome man.

A girl who picked a rosebud on Midsummer's Day, wrapped it in white paper and hid it away until Christmas Day, would wear it to church if it remained fresh, and the man who took it away from her would be her husband. In some places it was customary to place a white rose on the grave of a virgin, a red one on the grave of someone distinguished for their kindness. However, in parts of Italy the red rose is an emblem of early death, and it's an evil omen to scatter its petals on the ground. Briars are said to spring up on the graves of lovers, growing towards each other before eventually becoming entwined. 'The Devil', wrote John Ruskin, 'is mortally afraid of roses and crocuses, of roses, that is, growing wild,' adding wistfully, 'What lovely hedges of them there were in the lane leading from Dulwich College up to Windmill Hill in my aunt's time.'

The wild rose's local names include hedgy pedgies, puckies, choops and nippernails

Rose-petal sandwiches make an elegant alternative to cucumber sandwiches, and in Tudor times people made mead with the scented leaves of the eglantine, mixed with herbs and honey. From earliest times rose hips have been used to make tarts and pies: 'The fruit when it is ripe maketh most pleasant meats and banqueting dishes, as tarts and the such like; the making thereof I commit to the cunning cooke, and teeth to eat them in the man's mouth,' writes Gerard. Rose hips feature in a recipe for mead drunk by the Elizabethans, described as giving a feeling of 'exhilaration'. If fairies eat a rose hip and turn anti-clockwise three times, they disappear. To become visible again they must eat another one and turn clockwise three times.

There's an old country saying, 'Many hops and haws, many frosts and snaws', and John Clare used rose hips (as well as hawthorn berries) as a weather indicator:

The thorns and briars, vermilion hue
Now full of hips and haws are seen
If village prophecies be true
They prove that winter will be keen.

Rose hips are a vital source of food for wintering birds. In the past, however, country children sometimes got there first, loving to split them open and use the hairy seeds as itching powder.

Medicinally, rose petals have been used as remedies for diarrhoea, coughs and colds, flu, lethargy and painful joints. They can be eaten raw to increase circulation and relieve depression, and a cream made from rose petals does wonders for the complexion – if you can afford it, rose being among the most costly of essential oils. Rose oil, fiendishly expensive as it is, soothes irritated and chapped skin, and in aromatherapy is used to treat nervous tension and depression. Rose water was commonly prescribed for eye inflammations and to strengthen the heart.

Rose hip seeds are diuretic and were used to cure urinary-tract disorders, and are mildly laxative in a tea. They are an important source of vitamin C, and were widely used during the Second World War to make a syrup for ailing children. Homemade rose-hip tea sweetened with honey is an invigorating tonic, and since rose hips are astringent and expectorant, they were used in stomach complaints as well as for coughs and chest ailments, as well as acne, gum and teeth problems, and bleeding. In the Middle Ages, Robin's pincushion or bedeguar galls were highly esteemed for their astringency, and ensured a sound night's sleep if you put one under your pillow.

The island of Rhodes gets its name from roses cultivated there from wild varieties, *rhodon* being Ancient Greek for 'red'. Pliny called Britain 'Albion' because it was covered with pale wild roses, the white *R. arvensis* and the dog rose, *R. canina*, so-called because of the supposed ability of the roots to cure rabies and the bites of 'madde dogges'. Pliny said it got its name from a root, which cured a soldier of the Praetorian guard of hydrophobia, so the term 'dog' is not necessarily derogatory as it often is when applied to useless plants.

The wild rose's local names include hedgy pedgies, puckies, choops and nippernails.

SWEET BRIAR
Rosa rubiginosa

DOG ROSE
Rosa canina

WOOD ANEMONE

Anemone nemorosa

The wild anemone, a member of the buttercup family, is a 'windflower' flourishing in windy places. Pliny maintained that as a 'daughter of the wind' it flowers only when the wind blows, usually appearing during the first gales of March. In wet weather, the flowers of wood anemone droop to protect stamens from the rain: as a flower of the fairies these downturned petals (which are actually the sepals) are said to provide shelter for elves.

In the language of flowers anemone means 'forsaken'. According to a Greek legend, Zephyr, the west wind, fell in love with the nymph Anemone. In a fit of jealousy the goddess Chloris, equivalent to the Roman goddess Flora, transformed her into a flower and left her to the tender mercies of the north wind Boreas. Zephyr, unable to win her love, shook her roughly, opening her nodding flowers.

The anemone gave rise to another love-myth: mortally wounded by a wild boar, Adonis lay in the bloodstained grass. There he was discovered by Venus who, overcome with grief, swore that her lover should live forever as a flower. As she wandered through the woods weeping, anemones sprang up where her tears fell, as remembered by Shakespeare in 'Venus and Adonis':

> *A purple flower sprung up, chequer'd with white:*
> *Resembling well his pale cheeks, and the blood*
> *Which in round drops upon their whiteness stood.*

Ever since, the flower was sacred to Venus and inspired love. When Oberon commands Puck, in *A Midsummer Night's Dream*, to anoint Titania's eyes with the juice of a flower, it's the anemone that makes her fall in love with the first creature she sets eyes on when she wakes up, although folklore has it that to dream of wood anemone means your lover is unfaithful and should be put aside in favour of a better.

In the language of flowers anemone means 'forsaken'

Carpets of wood anemones flower towards the end of winter all over the British Isles, apart from Orkney and Shetland. In East Anglia they are particularly associated with ancient woodland. They flourish in damp, coppiced woods, in meadows and along hedgerows, spreading slowly, at a rate of only 6 feet a century, by root reproduction. The leaves have delicate stalks with beautiful, deeply lobed leaves. The solitary white flowers are delicate stars, often tinged with pale red or mauve at the bases. These produce no nectar, but are pollinated by bees, bumblebees and a variety of flies. Their musty smell led to a local name of smell fox, and in some countries people believed the air to be so bad where wild anemones grow that the unpleasant smell caused sickness. In fact the plant contains proto-anemonin, and is poisonous, although you can safely press a poultice of the leaves to your forehead to cure a headache.

Their musty smell led to a local name of smell fox

The Ancient Greeks maintained that everyone should pick the first anemone they see in the spring while saying, 'I pick you for a remedy against disease'. The flower was then wrapped in a scarlet cloth until the person began to feel ill, when it was tied around their neck or arm to protect them. This superstition extended to England, according to a ballad:

> *The first spring-blown anemone she in his doublet wove*
> *To keep him safe from pestilence wherever he should rove.*

The generic name derives from the Greek *anemos*, 'wind', and *nemorosa* means 'shady', from the habitat. Local names include thunderbolt (since picking it causes a thunderstorm), granny's nightcap, moggie nightgown, Moll of the woods, moon flower, silver bells, drops of snow, Candlemas caps (Candlemas falling on 2 February, an association the wood anemone shares with the snowdrop), moon flower and thimbleweed.

WORMWOOD

Artemisia absinthium

Wormwood is one of the biblical bitter herbs, mentioned in the Books of Proverbs, Job and Jeremiah. The plant sprang from tracks made by the serpent in Eden, and came to represent calamity and profound sorrow. In the Book of Revelations of St John the Divine, 'The third angel blew his trumpet, and a great star fell from heaven, blazing like a torch, and it fell on a third of the rivers and on the springs of water. The name of the star is wormwood. A third of the waters became wormwood, and many died from the water, because it was made bitter.' In *Hamlet*, Shakespeare used the phrase 'Wormwood, wormwood' to signify the bitterness of somebody's words, and in Russia it represents an unpalatable truth that deluded people need to accept.

Conversely, wormwood is used as a love potion, or burned as incense to heighten psychic powers – or even hung up on a car mirror as a lucky amulet. A strange snippet of folklore has it that if you rub the hands of an infant with the juice of wormwood before it is three months old, it will never be too hot or too cold throughout its life. To dream of wormwood is an omen of good luck and domestic happiness.

In eighteenth-century England, wormwood was used in beer instead of hops, and made into wine. In Morocco, wormwood is sometimes added to mint tea. Most famously it went into vermouth, a wine flavoured with aromatic herbs and alleged to be a mental restorative (the word vermouth means 'preserver of the mind'). Wormwood is a principal flavouring ingredient of absinthe, the highly addictive and dangerous drink beloved of artists and poets of the nineteenth century, which can be fatal in large quantities.

With its heavy scent, wormwood contains the vermifuge santonin and is an effective insect repellent: deterring both fleas and moths, it got its name from this traditional use. Bunches of wormwood were often hung up in cottages and put into drawers and clothes cupboards. You can make an effective plant spray against garden pests by infusing wormwood with rainwater. Plant this handsome wild flower as a companion plant to suppress weeds, since its roots secrete substances that inhibit growth of surrounding plants – but don't for this reason let it into the vegetable patch!

In herbal medicine, wormwood is a proven stomachic, antiseptic, antispasmodic, febrifuge and carminative. Dioscorides used it to cure worms, and a tincture was prescribed for nervous disorders. It is strongly antimicrobial, especially against pathogenic bacteria. The pure oil is poisonous, but the correctly prescribed dosage of wormwood can be extremely beneficial. Local names include vermouth and wormod.

> *Its powers are famous,*
> *Its effectiveness proven. It tames a raging thirst; fever*

It banishes. If, besides, your head should suddenly start to
Throb and throb with pain, if fits of fainting worry you,
Seek its help:
Boil the bitter stem of a plant
In leaf, tip the brew into an ample basin
And pour it over the top of your head. Then having bathed
Your soft hair with the liquid make a garland of leaves
(Do not forget this) and put it on, so that the bandage
Gently binds your hair and holds the warmth in it.
A few hours later – not many – you will be marvelling
At this yet further proof at the healing powers of wormwood.
WALAFRID STRABO, *HORTULUS*, C. AD840

Wormwood is a member of a large plant family: there are hundreds of artemisias worldwide, among them mugwort, southernwood and tarragon. They are all aromatic, and attract numerous butterflies and moths. A few are grown as ornamental plants, but mostly they are found in the wild in well-drained, often sandy soils, in full sun.

One of the most familiar artemisias, tarragon (*A. dracunculus*), is native to Russia but cultivated worldwide. In France it's known as *herbe au dragon*. The 'little dragon' had the power to heal dragon bites, and some country people knew it as dragon mugwort. Famous as a culinary herb, tarragon also attracts love and affection. Known to stimulate digestion, it had a place in the country medicine cabinet as a mild sedative, to treat stings, snake bites or the bites of rabid dogs. Or, chew a piece of tarragon root to cure toothache.

The active principal artemisinin isolated from annual wormwood, *A. annua*, is the starting compound in antimalarial drugs. It has the most rapid action of all current drugs against malaria, and is standard treatment worldwide. *A. annua* tea made from the dried leaves and buds can be drunk as an effective prophylactic against malaria, and you can make your own safely, and for free. *A. annua* is also known as sweet wormwood, sweet Annie or sweet sagewort.

YARROW

Achillea millefolium

On the advice of healer-centaur Chiron, Achilles applied yarrow to the wounds of his friend Telemachus at the siege of Troy, and the plant staunched the bleeding, hence *Achillea*. *Millefolium* describes the many divisions of the leaves, and 'yarrow' itself comes either from the Greek *hiera*, 'holy herb', or from an Anglo-Saxon word for 'healer' (or possibly both). The leaves are antiseptic too, so stuffing yarrow into a wound not only stops the bleeding but helps to prevent infection. Among a myriad of local names are carpenter's weed or grass (from its use in stemming the flow of blood from chisel wounds), also woundwort, soldiers woundwort, nosebleed – since it stops them – sneezewort, old man's pepper, milfoil and yarroway.

Yarrow has supernatural powers against enchantments, and for the Irish it's one of the herbs of midsummer magic to be hung up around

266

the house on St John's Eve, 23 June, to fend off evil. If you wear it, you'll be safe from danger and free from fear; if you hang it on a cradle the baby will be protected; and yarrow strewn over your threshold will keep witches away. However, it was in some places dedicated to the Devil and known to some as Devil's nettle, used by witches in their spells and incantations (a witch was tried for using it as recently as the seventeenth century).

> *To dream of yarrow means that you will shortly hear of something that will give you great pleasure*

To dream of yarrow means that you will shortly hear of something that will give you great pleasure. Yarrow was used in love divination: there was an East Anglian custom for young girls to tickle the insides of their nostrils with a yarrow leaf, and recite,

> *Yarroway, yarroway, bear a white blow,*
> *If my love love me, my nose will bleed now.*

Lovesick wenches would pick it and sing,

> *Thou pretty herb of Venus-Tree*
> *Thy true name is Yarrow;*
> *Now who my bosom friend must be*
> *Pray tell thou me tomorrow.*

The delicate pink-tinged white (or wholly pink) flowers were often used in bridal bouquets and garlands at country weddings. A local name of Venus tree indicates its magical powers over love: if eaten at a wedding, the couple would love one another for at least seven years.

Not merely a woundwort, yarrow was regarded as a cure-all, and remained in European pharmacopoeias until the early nineteenth century. Its antiseptic qualities were used for stomach, kidney, heart and skin complaints. As a febrifuge it was a remedy for fevers and influenza. The flowers were recommended 'boiled and mixed with cayenne pepper, as a remedy for cold in the chest'. Banckes's *Herball* of 1525 instructs, 'Alas for him that may not hold his meat, [let him] stamp this herbe with wine and drink it warm.' Yarrow tea was said to be good for melancholy and colds, to maintain hair colour and stop it falling out: Linnaeus recommended it for rheumatism and the fresh leaf can alleviate toothache. In modern homeopathic medicine it is employed as a stimulant and haemostatic.

Yarrow has been used in Scandinavia for brewing beer, and the leaves, which produce a yellow dye, can also be smoked as a substitute tobacco, or dried for snuff. The plant provides food for numerous moths including the mullein wave, the yarrow plume and the tawny speckled pug. The counting of 49 yarrow sticks is the traditional method of divining the *I Ching*, ancient Chinese 'Book of Changes'. Local names include thousand-leaved grass, bloodwort and staunch-grass.

It is not only in the seed or flower but in the whole plant, stems, leaves, roots that we discover, if we but lower our heads for a moment over their humble work, many traces of a lively and shrewd intelligence ... showing that the faculty of adaptation and intelligent progress is not the exclusive domain of the human race ... We would know very few signs or expressions of happiness if we did not know the flower ... its power and beauty ...

Maurice Maeterlinck, *The Intelligence of Flowers*, 1907

Acknowledgements and Thanks

I owe a great debt to Matthew Oates for championing this book
with the National Trust: thank you Matthew for your enthusiasm,
and thanks to the National Trust's publisher Katie Bond for steering
it through.

For much of the original material on which the work is based I
am indebted to botanist and artist Molly Hyde. After illustrating my
Hedgerow Cookery (Penguin, 1980), she bequeathed to me her lifelong
collection of notes on botany and folklore, which have been a constant
presence in my work ever since. I began to collate them with the
idea of one day writing a book based on the natural histories of wild
flowers and trees. I owe thanks to BBC Radio Cambridgeshire for a
regular slot for several years, which allowed me to hold forth on some
of the plants and their relevance to our everyday lives. Features based
on this work have been published in *Country Life* and *The Countryman*
magazines, acknowledged with gratitude. Thanks too to Mina Gorji
who invited me to speak on John Clare's wild flowers at the inaugural
conference of the Centre for John Clare Studies at Cambridge
University in 2014. Sharing conversations about wild flowers with
Ronald Blythe has been a recent and unexpected pleasure, and I am
grateful to Jeremy Mynott for his valuable editorial comments on
my Introduction. Thanks too to my many friends and companions
along the way, including James Parry for his knowledgeable company
on many a wildlife walk, and to all the inspiring people I have met
through New Networks for Nature: with especial thanks to Mike
Toms and John Fanshawe for inviting me to give a presentation on
Richard Jefferies and the metaphysics of wild flowers. And thanks to
Peter Taylor and editor Lucy Smith at Pavilion Books for the pleasure
of working with them, and for producing a book which reflects the
beauty of this great passion of mine.

Page 12:
Peter Marren, 'Harvests of Beauty: the conservation of Hay
Meadows,' British Wildlife Publishing 6:235–43 (1995). Reproduced
by kind permission of British Wildlife Publishing.

Pages 12, 14:
George Peterken, *Meadows*, used by permission of Bloomsbury
Publishing Plc.

Page 17:
Roger Deakin, *Notes from Walnut Tree Farm* (London: Hamish
Hamilton, 2008). Reproduced by permission of Penguin Books Ltd.

Page 83:
Lyrics from the Chinese, translated by Helen Waddell. Reproduced by
kind permission of Margaret Louise Anson of Helen Waddell's Estate.

SELECT BIBLIOGRAPHY

Arber, Agnes, *Herbals* (Cambridge University Press, 1912)

von Bingen, Hildegard, *Physica*, transl. Priscilla Throop (Healing Arts Press Vermont, 1998)

Blythe, Ronald, *Outsiders: A Book of Garden Friends* (Black Dog Books, 2008)

Bruton-Seal, Matthew and Julie, *Hedgerow Medicine* (Merlin Unwin, 2009)

    The Herbalist's Bible (Merlin Unwin, 2014)

Chevalier, Andrew, *Encyclopedia of Medicinal Plants* (Dorling Kindersley, 1997)

Clare, John, *The Natural History Prose Writings*, ed. Margaret Grainger (Clarendon, 1983)

    The Major Works, ed. Robinson and Powell (Oxford University Press, 2004)

Coats, Alice, *Flowers and their Histories* (Hutton, 1956)

Cocker, Mark and Mabey, Richard, *Flora Britannica* (Sinclair Stevenson, 1996)

Culpeper, Nicholas, *Culpeper's Complete Herbal* (Foulsham, undated)

Deakin, Roger, *Notes from Walnut Tree Farm* (Penguin, 2009)

Fitter, Richard and Alastair, and Blamey, Marjorie, *Wild Flowers of Britain and Northern Europe* (Collins, 1974)

Folkard, Richard, *Plant Lore, Legends and Lyrics* (Sampson, Searle and Rivington, 1884)

Garrard, Ian and Streeter, David, *The Wild Flowers of the British Isles* (Macmillan, 1983)

Gerard, John, *The Herbal* (Dover Publications, 1975)

Grieve, Mrs, *A Modern Herbal* (Jonathan Cape, 1931)

Grigson, Geoffrey, *A Dictionary of Plant Names* (Allen Lane, 1974)

    The Englishman's Flora (Paladin, 1958)

Hallé, Francis, *In Praise of Plants* (Timber Press, 2002)

Hensel, Wolfgang, *Medicinal Plants of Britain and Europe* (A&C Black, 2007)

Hole, Christina, *Encyclopedia of Superstitions* (Hutchinson, 1980)

Hopkins, Gerard Manley, *The Major Works* (Oxford World Classics, 2009)

Hyde, Molly, *Hedgerow Plants* (Shire Publications, 1976)

Jefferies, Richard, *The Story of my Heart* (Green Books, 1883)

    The Nature Diaries and Note-books (Grey Walls Press, 1948)

    At Home on the Earth, ed. Jeremy Hooker (Green Books, 2001)

    The Open Air (Echo Library, 2005)

Language of Flowers, transl. from the French (Saunders and Otley)

Leighton, Clare, *Country Matters* (Gollancz, 1937)

    Four Hedges (Gollancz, 1937)

Lubbock, Sir John, *British Wild Flowers Considered in Relation to Insects* (Macmillan, 1893)

Mabey, Richard, *Plants with a Purpose* (Collins, 1977)

McLeod, R. D., *Keys to the Names of British Plants* (Pitman, 1952)

Messegué, Maurice, *Health Secrets of Plants and Herbs* (Collins, 1975)

Palaiseul, Jean, *Grandmother's Secrets* (Penguin, 1973)

Parkinson, John, *Paradisus in Sole* (Dover, 1991)

Peterken, George, *Meadows* (British Wildlife, 2013)

Poisonous Plants, Bulletin 161 (HMSO, 1976)

Randall, Vernon, *Wild Flowers in Literature* (Scholartis Press, 1924)

Rohde, Eleanor, *The Old English Herbals* (Minerva, 1974)

Strabo, Walafrid, *Hortulus* (Stanton Press, 1924)

Thomas, R.S. Collected Poems 1945–1990 (W&N, 2000)

Thompson, Dorothy B., Griswold, Ralph E., *Garden Lore of Ancient Athens* (Princeton Press, 1963)

Thompson, William, *Healing Plants* (Macmillan, 1980)

Traherne, Thomas, *Centuries* (Clarendon Press, 1975)

Turner, William, *The Names of Herbes* (Classic Reprint, 2015)

Walton, Izaak, *The Compleat Angler* (Oxford University Press, 2014)

Zohary, Michael, *Plants of the Bible* (Cambridge University Press, 1982)

INDEX

Hill, Sir John 43, 157, 186
hoary 70
hogweed 29, 147–8, *147*
Homogyne alpina 78
honeysuckle 149–51, *149*
hop *152*, 153–5
Hope flowers 73, 112, 221
Hopkins, Gerard Manley 15, 40
Horace 175–6
Humulus lupulus 152, 153–5
Hyacinthoides
  H. agraphis 42
  H. hispanica 41
  H. non-scripta 18, 40–3
Hypericum
  H. androsaenum 229
  H. calycinum 229
  H. perforatum 226–9, *226*
Hypochoeris radicata 140

Inula
  I. helenium 102, 103–5
  I. salicina 111

Jefferies, Richard 11, 13, 18, 37, 50,
  131

knapweed *156*, 157

lady's bedstraw 127, 135, *158*,
  159–60
lady's mantle 161–3, *161*
lady's smock 164–5, *164*
Lamiastrum galeobdolon 100, 101
Lamium 99–101

L. album 99, 100, *101*
L. amplexicaule 100
L. luteum 100
L. maculatum 101
L. purpureum 100
Language of Flowers 25, 37, 50, 70,
  74, 83, 118, 149, 154, 169, 175,
  197, 221, 223, 237, 240, 247, 255,
  260, 261
Lapwing 151
Leontodon 138, 139–40
  L. autumnalis 139–40, *143*
  L. hispidus 140, *142*
lesser burdock 166–7, *166*
lesser celandine 10, 168–9, *168*
Lightning plants 47, 57, 131, 164,
  196, 209, 241
Linnaeus, Carl 41, 151, 268
Linnet 131
Lonicera periclymenum 149–51, *149*
lords and ladies 42, 170–2, *170*
Lotus corniculatus 36–7, *36*
Luck, good 61, 73, 89, 94, 113, 121,
  125, 145, 202, 203, 223, 264
Luck, bad 94, 118, 137, 145, 179,
  200, 203, 237
lungwort 173–4
Lychnis coronaria 57
Lyte, Henry 80, 135, 188

mallow 175–7, *175*
Malva
  M. moschata 175–7, *175*
  M. sylvestris 175–7, *175*
marshmallow 177

277

279